BMAT Past Paper
Worked Solutions

ISBN 978-0-9932311-4-8

Published by *RAR Medical Services Limited*
www.uniadmissions.co.uk
info@uniadmissions.co.uk
Tel: 0203 375 6294

BMAT is a registered trademark of Cambridge Assessment, which was not involved in the production of, and does not endorse, this book. The authors and publisher are not affiliated with BMAT or Cambridge Assessment. The answers and explanations given in this book are purely the opinions of the authors rather than an official set of answers.

The information offered in this book is purely advisory and any advice given should be taken within this context. As such, the publishers and authors accept no liability whatsoever for the outcome of any applicant's BMAT performance, the outcome of any university applications or for any other loss. Although every precaution has been taken in the preparation of this book, the publisher and author assume no responsibility for errors or omissions of any kind. Neither is any liability assumed for damages resulting from the use of information contained herein. This does not affect your statutory rights.

BMAT Past Paper
Worked Solutions

Rohan Agarwal

UniAdmissions

THE BASICS

What are BMAT Past Papers?

Thousands of students take the BMAT exam in November each year. These exam papers are then released online to help future students prepare for the exam. Before 2013, these papers were not publically available meaning that students had to rely on the specimen papers and other resources for practice. However, since their release in 2013, BMAT past papers have become an invaluable resource in any student's preparation.

Where can I get BMAT Past Papers?

This book does not include BMAT past paper questions because it would be over 1,000 pages long! However, BMAT past papers for the last 10 years are available for free from the official BMAT website (www.admissionstestingservice.org/for-test-takers/bmat). To save you the hassle of downloading lots of files, we've put them all into one easy-to-access folder for you at **www.uniadmissions.co.uk/bmat-past-papers**.

At the time of publication, the 2014 past paper has not been released so this book only contains answers for 2003 – 2013. An updated version will be made available once the 2014 paper is released.

How should I use BMAT Past Papers?

BMAT Past papers are one the best ways to prepare for the BMAT. Careful use of them can dramatically boost your scores in a short period of time. The way you use them will depend on your learning style and how much time you have until the exam date but here are some general pointers:

➢ 4-6 weeks of preparation is usually sufficient for the majority of students.
➢ Students generally improve in section 2 more quickly than section 1 so if you have limited time, focus on section 2.

> ➤ The BMAT syllabus changed in 2009 so if you find seemingly strange questions in the earlier papers, ensure you check to see if the topic is still on the specification.
> ➤ Similarly, there is little point doing essays before 2009 as they are significantly different in style. We've included plans for them in this book for completeness in any case.

How should I prepare for the BMAT?

Although this is a cliché, the best way to prepare for the exam is to start early – ideally by September at the latest. If you're organised, you can follow the schema below:

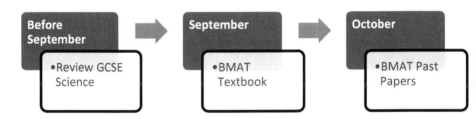

This paradigm allows you to minimise gaps in your knowledge before you start practicing with BMAT style questions in a textbook. In general, aim to get a textbook that has lots of practice questions e.g. *The Ultimate BMAT Guide* (**www.uniadmissions.co.uk/bmat-book**) – this allows you to rapidly identify any weaknesses that you might have e.g. Newtonian mechanics, simultaneous equations etc.

Finally, it's then time to move onto past papers. The number of BMAT papers you can do will depend on the time you have available but you should try to do at least 2009 – 2014 once.

If you have time, do 2003- 2008 once (ignore section 3). If you find that you've exhausted all BMAT resources and have time left, go through the 2009 – 2014 papers again. Practice really does make perfect!

How should I use this book?

This book is designed to accelerate your learning from BMAT past papers. Avoid the urge to have this book open alongside a past paper you're seeing for the first time. The BMAT is difficult because of the intense time pressure it puts you under – the best way of replicating this is by doing past papers under strict exam conditions (no half measures!). Don't start out by doing past papers (see previous page) as this 'wastes' papers.

Once you've finished, take a break and then mark your answers. Then, review the questions that you got wrong followed by ones which you found tough/spent too much time on. This is the best way to learn and with practice, you should find yourself steadily improving. You should keep a track of your scores on the next page so you can track your progress.

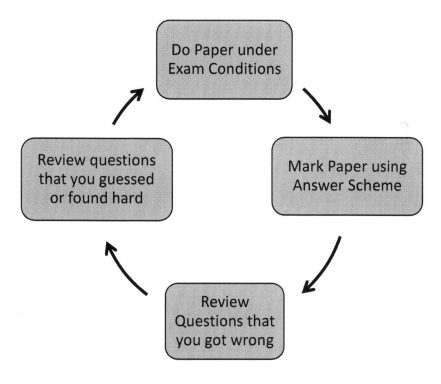

Scoring Tables

Use these to keep a record of your scores – you can then easily see which paper you should attempt next (always the one with the lowest score).

SECTION 1	1st Attempt	2nd Attempt	3rd Attempt
2003			
2004			
2005			
2006			
2007			
2008			
2009			
2010			
2011			
2012			
2013			
2014			

SECTION 2	1st Attempt	2nd Attempt	3rd Attempt
2003			
2004			
2005			
2006			
2007			
2008			
2009			
2010			
2011			
2012			
2013			
2014			

Extra Practice

If you're blessed with a good memory, you might remember the answers to certain questions in the past papers – making it less useful to repeat them again. If you want to tackle extra mock papers which are fully up-to-date then check out **www.uniadmissions.co.uk/bmat-practice-papers** for **4** x full mock papers with worked solutions.

These are normally £60 but as thanks for purchasing this book, you can get them for £40 instead. Just enter "*BMATWS20*" at checkout.

SECTION 1	1st Attempt	2nd Attempt	3rd Attempt
Practice Paper A			
Practice Paper B			
Practice Paper C			
Practice Paper D			

SECTION 2	1st Attempt	2nd Attempt	3rd Attempt
Practice Paper A			
Practice Paper B			
Practice Paper C			
Practice Paper D			

2003

Section 1

Question 1: E

There is a large increase in volume for a small increase in depth at either end, and a small increase in volume for a large increase in depth in the middle, which can only correspond to E.

Question 2: C

The argument is that ready meals should have health warnings, and the reason is because they are unhealthy. The fact that people are unaware strengthens the link between the evidence and the conclusion

Question 3: B

Sum all the rows and columns. 1 row and 1 column will be incorrect, and where these meet will be the incorrect value. Summing the year 8s gives 150, not 145 and summing the cars gives 107, not 102. Thus year 8s going by car is an incorrect value (33).

Question 4: C

The passage states that the new financial support for students must be repaid, and states that students from poorer families are more likely to be deterred by the prospect of debt. The link between these 2 can be inferred, suggesting the government's changes may deter poorer students more, said in C.

Question 5: 109

Cabbages $= n^2 + 9 = (n+1)^2 - 12$. Rearrange, and the n^2 cancel to leave $2n = 20$
$n = 10$, cabbages $= 109$

Question 6: D

Here, the conclusion is within the middle of the argument: 'it may be undemocratic by favouring some political parties more than others.' This is paraphrased by D.

Question 7: A

A surgery session was on average 140 minutes, and each appointment is made 10 minutes apart (and the average length of a consultation is usually 10 minutes), so $140/10 = 14$ patients would be seen in an average session.

Question 8: 27

140 x 8.5 (surgery a week) + 408 = 1598 (~1600)
1600/60 = 80/3 = 26.6 = 27 to the nearest hour

Question 9: C

10000000 people / 5000 doctors = 2000 patients per doctor.
155 seen a week, 155 x 50 = 7750 total visits a year
7750/2000 = ~4 visits per year

Question 10: D

We know the average length of a surgery session is 165 mins, and with less doctors, this will have to increase - we can thus rule out A, B and C. To work out the proportion - 165 x 5 = 4.5 x new length of surgery needed. New length needed = 183 mins.

Question 11: A

We can probably get to A without having to do any calculations. We can rule out B - 1 second extra per consultation is unlikely to contribute most to the rise. The average time spent on home visits per week is less than the average length of a surgery session (of which there are several a week), hence the length of surgery sessions must contribute more. The average length of a home visit is irrelevant because we already have the time spent on home visits per week.

Question 12: A

The average numbers of patients seen per week are 135 and 155 respectively - shown by A.

Question 13: B

If x people are on the bus...
$2x/3$ people stay on at the first stop, $4x/9$ at the second and $8x/27$ at the third. $8x/27 = 8$, thus $x = 27$.

Question 14: E

This is another causation/correlation BMAT question. The assumption is that excessive Internet use causes isolation and obesity, but no evidence of a causal link.

Question 15: C

Firstly, every team will play two matches against the other 5 teams in their pool. So team A must play B, C, D, E and F twice which is 10 matches, B must play C, D, E and F which is 8 matches (don't repeat A), etc. This makes a total of $10+8+6+4+2=30$ in the pool, so a total of 60 with 2 pools. Also, each team plays each of the other teams in the other pool once, giving $6 \times 6 = 36$ extra matches (there are no repeats here). There is also the final. $60 + 36 + 1 = 97$ matches.

Question 16: C

The line y=5 is only shown in A, B and C, and out of these y=2x only in A and C. Comparing A and C, only C shows when y is greater than 2x, whereas A shows y is less than 2x.

Question 17: B

Again, another causation/correlation question. The finding only gives a correlation, which is said by B. None of the other claims can be justified.

Question 18: 5

15 take the BMAT, 13 take Biology so 2 don't take Biology. The 2 that don't must be taking Chemistry, Physics and Maths. We also know that 3 people take Chemistry, Biology, Physics and Maths - 3+2=5. We can assume all 5 of these are boys because we are looking to maximise the number of boys.

Question 19: D

The actual time doesn't matter here. Julie's clock is one hour ahead of Clare, so she will arrive 1 hour before.

Question 20: B

The argument is that we should promote seeking advice at an earlier stage. However, if early consultation for minor symptoms incurs high costs in doctors' time then this weakens the argument.

Question 21: 7.2 seconds

The cheetah runs 50km/h faster than the Zebra and is 100m (0.1km) behind. Time = distance/speed, so 0.1/50 = 0.002 hours. To convert this into seconds, times by 3600, which gives 7.2.

Question 22: E

It had to be occupied in AD157 or there would not be any coins of this date - thus E is the only one that is definitely true.

Question 23: B

The conclusion is that the habitats of wading birds will inevitably decline, and this is due to peat. However, the assumption is that people will carry on using peat despite the alternatives. A, C, D and E are not necessarily assumed.

Question 24: C

The Fair-E coefficient is said to represent the degree of inequality in income distribution, and as this has increased, we can conclude that income inequality has not been reduced.
A is not correct as we know nothing about overall income of people.
B is not true - chart 1 suggests an increase in household income for low earners.
D is not true as we do not know about standard of living.
E is not true because we don't know anything about 'real wealth'.

Question 25: D

Chart 1 shows that for those with below average incomes, there has been a net gain. The only way this could happen with the Fair-E coefficient could have increased is if the pre-tax incomes of the rich have risen even more than the poor.
We cannot say changes are due to government fiscal policy (A), B is too general and claims too much, the use of 'better off' is too vague in C and E cannot be concluded as poverty is not mentioned.

Question 26: E

1 is correct - the income increase of the poor is less than it could have been as seen in the data.

2 could definitely be correct and we have already explored the idea that the incomes at the top end may have increased more than those at the bottom end.

3 could also increase the Fair-E coefficient while taxes and benefits change for the poor.

Question 27: C

The degree of inequality is measured by the Fair-E coefficient. Poland (0.2), Ruritania (0.35), USA (0.4) and Panama (0.6) is the order.

Question 28: B

Again, the problem is that the argument confuses cause with correlation. 2 factors may be correlated, but the causality can be either way around, or they may be linked by another factor. Thus B is the correct answer.

Question 29: E

The probability of it being yellow or blue is 70%, so 70/3% yellow and 140/3% blue. We can say there are 3 red, 7/3 yellow and 14/3 blue, but obviously there must be whole numbers. If we times them all by 3, there are 9 red, 7 yellow and 14 blue, totalling 30.

Question 30: C

1 is correct - 30% work, at least some of the time, in the commercial sector, which covers doctors working in both and the commercial sector alone. Thus, some doctors must work in the public service only.

2 is also correct - 70% work solely in the public sector, whereas 30% work in either both or just commercial.

3 cannot be deduced - we don't know how much time doctors spend at each service.

Question 31: A & C

Express each one as an inequality - a $\leq$ s, s $<$ a, s $\geq$ a and a $\geq$ s. From this you can see A and C are equivalent. If this is not obvious to you, try considering whether Anne can be older than Susan, whether Anne and Susan can be the same age or whether Anne can be younger than Susan for each one.

Question 32: E

The conclusion is that the government must act quickly to plan for changes in holiday patterns, but the assumption here is that these changes will be more than short term.

Question 33: D

B>D and C>A to start with. D goes back 1 place so cannot start last, and B goes up 1 place so cannot start first. Thus, we can deduce that originally the order is CBDA. After the swap the order is BCAD.

Question 34: C

At the moment we have 10 parts water to 1 part concentrate, so we need to add concentrate, ruling out A and B. Test the other ones. If we add 10cm concentrate we now have 400cm water and 50cm concentrate, which is the correct 8:1 part dilution.

Question 35: C

Determine the net change for each year e.g. 800 lost for year 1. We can immediately rule out A B and D as they begin with an increase rather than a decrease. F doesn't decrease by 800 in the first year so is also wrong. We are left with C and E. E is not correct because there is an increase between years 2 and 3, so C must be correct.

Question 36: B

If 455AD is year 9, then year 72 is 455 + 63 = 518AD.

Question 37: C

We know that Gildas was born in the year of the battle of Badon so if we knew his birth date we could confirm the date of the battle.

Question 38: B

Year 93 would be 539AD in the Welsh Annals. But if this was too late by 28 years, then the battle would have been in 511AD.

Question 39: 506AD

Death of King Maelgwn was in 549AD. If Gildas was 43 at this date, the battle of Badon would be as late as possible: 549 - 43 = 506AD.

Question 40: C

The Welsh Annals give information suggesting Gildas wrote his book after the King's death, which is only shown by C.

END OF SECTION

Section 2

Question 1: B

➤ Starch is partially digested in the mouth by amylase.
➤ Proteins are digested in the stomach via proteases like pepsin.
➤ Fats are only digested in the small intestine.

Question 2: E

Mass of 8×10^6 uranium atoms $= 4 \times 10^{-25} \times 8 \times 10^6$

$32 \times 10^{-19} kg = 32 \times 10^{-13} mg$

$= 3.2 \times 10^{-12} mg$

Question 3: 2, 9, 6

The quickest way to do these type of questions is via algebraic equations. If you're unfamiliar with this approach then see the chemistry chapter in *The Ultimate BMAT Guide*.

For Carbon: 3a = 6. Hence, **a =2**

For Hydrogen: 6a = 2c; 12 = 2c. Hence, **c = 6**

For Oxygen: 2b = 12 + c; 2b = 12 + 6. Hence, **b = 9**

Question 4: B

Since the pivot is located in the middle of the bar, we can ignore the bar's weight. For the bar to balance:

$Moments\ clockwise\ =\ Moments\ anti-clockwise$
$500 \times 0.2\ =\ 0.4 \times 200\ +\ 200x$
$100\ =\ 80\ +\ 200x$
$x = \frac{20}{200} = 0.1m$

Question 5: D
Don't get confused – this is easy! At pH 5, methyl orange would be yellow, bromothymol blue would be yellow and phenolphthalein would be colourless. Thus, the solution would be yellow.

Question 6: 76.8 kJ

$$Weight = mass \; x \; g$$

$$Thus, the \; horse's \; mass \; = \frac{6000}{10} = 600 \; kg$$

$$E_k = \frac{1}{2} mv^2 = \frac{1}{2} x \; 600 \; x \; 16^2$$

$$= 300 \; x \; 256$$

$$= 76,800 \; J \; = 76.8 \; kJ$$

Question 7: B

This is no longer on the specification. Oestrogen reaches its highest level in the days prior to ovulation. Hence phase B is the correct answer.

Question 8: A, C, B and D

Don't make this more complex than it needs to be by using algebra! Resistors in parallel have a lower overall resistance than the same resistors in series. Thus A has the lowest resistance and D has the highest resistance. B only has one resistor in each branch but C has two resistors in the top branch. Thus, C has a higher resistance than B.

Question 9: B

Number of moles of $H_2 = \frac{9}{2} = 4.5$ moles

Number of moles of $N_2 = \frac{56}{28} = 2$ moles

Since 3 moles of H_2 react with 1 mole N_2, nitrogen gas is in excess.

The molar ratio between H_2 and NH_3 is 3:2 so:

4.5 moles of H_2 react with 3 moles of NH_3.

The mass of 3 moles of $NH_3 = 3 \times [14 + 3]$

$= 51g$

Question 10: B

This is just a simple exponential curve and thus is best shown by graph B. If you were unsure, you could substitute in some values and see what x is.

For example:
➤ When x = 0, y = 1 (ruling out A and C),
➤ When x = 1, y = 2 (ruling out D, as x and y increase together).

Question 11: A

Don't get confused, wavelength can change during refraction but the frequency of waves always stays the same for these phenomena.

Question 12: A

Succinic acid loses two hydrogen atoms to become fumaric acid. This is an example of an oxidation reaction.

Question 13: D

Rearrange the equation: $x^2 + 2x - 8 \geq 0$

Factorise: $(x - 2)(x + 4) \geq 0$

Remember that this is a quadratic inequality so requires a quick sketch to ensure you don't make a silly mistake with which way the sign is.

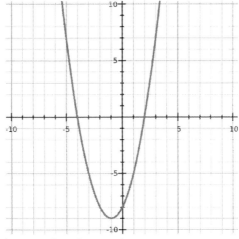

Thus, $y = 0$ when $x = 2$ and $x = -4$

$y > 0$ when $x > 2$ or $x < -4$

Thus, the solution is: $x \leq -4 \; and \; x \geq 2$

This is the same as $x^2 + 2x - 8 \geq 0$ which we can solve with an equals sign to get x = 2 and x = -4. To satisfy the original inequality we must have x ≥ 2 or x ≤ -4 (sub in numbers if unsure).

Question 14: 3, 4 and 5; E

Since 4 and 5 don't have the condition but 7 does, the disease is inherited in an autosomal recessive fashion. Thus, 4 and 5 must be heterozygotes. As 7 is affected, 3 must also be a heterozygote carrier.

Since 3 and 4 are heterozygotes, they have a 25% chance of having a child who has the disease or a 12.5% chance of having a girl with the disease.

	A	**a**
A	AA $\left(\frac{1}{4}\right)$	Aa $\left(\frac{1}{4}\right)$
a	Aa $\left(\frac{1}{4}\right)$	**aa** $\left(\frac{1}{4}\right)$

$Probability\ (Girl\ with\ disease) = P(Girl)x\ P(Disease)$

$$= \frac{1}{2}x\frac{1}{4} = \frac{1}{8}$$

Question 15: 4 minutes

The initial count rate was 120 (taking background into account) and ended with 15 counts after 12 minutes. There were 3 half-lives in this time (120 -> 60 -> 30 -> 15) so each has a time of 4 minutes.

Question 16: C

Reading off the graph, 136g of potassium chlorate dissolves in 200g of water at 70°C. Since only 80g was added, the full amount will be dissolved at 70°C.

The solution will become saturated once only 40g of potassium chlorate can be dissolved in every 100g of water. This takes place at 46°C.

The solubility at 20°C is 27g per 100g of water. Thus, as the solutions cools from 46°C to 20°C, 40 – 27 =13g of potassium chlorate will crystallise per 100g of water.

Since there is 200 g of water, a total of 13 x 2 = 26g of crystals will form.

Question 17: E

Some of the equations required for this question are now outside the BMAT Syllabus.

A. $Energy = Charge \; x \; Voltage. Thus, V = Joules/Coulombs$
B. $From \; Ohm's \; Law: V = IR$
C. $Since \; P = IV, V = \frac{P}{I}$
D. $Since \; P = IV \; and \; V = IR, P = \frac{V^2}{R}. Therefore, V = \sqrt{PR}$
E. It's not possible to manipulate equations to fit the given units.

Question 18: E, B, C, A and D

ADH travels through the vena cava to the right side of the heart, which pumps the blood through the pulmonary artery and to the lungs. The blood then returns via the pulmonary vein to left side of the heart. Blood then leaves through the aorta and travels to the kidney via the renal artery.

Question 19: C

$Frequency = \frac{5}{10^{-13}} = 5 \times 10^{13} Hz$

$Energy = f \times h = 5 \times 10^{13} \times 6.63 \times 10^{-34}$

$= 33.15 \times 10^{-21}$

$= 3.32 \times 10^{-20} J$

Question 20: C

The atom has 4 electrons in the outer shell so is in group 4. It has 2 electron shells and hence is in period 2.

Question 21: E

Simplify this by working from right to left, looking at each thing you pass and the direction it operates in. You need to know where the biceps and triceps attach to the arm, but this is GCSE level science knowledge. For the upward action, on the far right you have the fulcrum of the elbow joint, then working leftwards you have the attachment of the biceps which pulls upwards then much further on you reach the load in the hands acting downwards. This is analogous to diagram 3. Then working for the downward action, you firstly have the upwards pull of triceps, then the fulcrum and then finally the upwards effort of the load, hence diagram 5 is correct.

Question 22: E

Increasing the speed of coil rotation increases the frequency and amplitude of the A.C. as well as the output voltage.

Question 23: E

The alkali metals form ionic bonds by donating an electron. This electron is lost more easily if it is further away from the positively charged nucleus. Whilst A, B, C and D may be true, they don't explain the increase in reactivity.

Question 24: C

During expiration, the ribs move down and inwards; the diaphragm relaxes and becomes less concave (= more convex). This causes intra-thoracic volume to decrease and intra-thoracic pressure to increase.

Question 25: B

$$\left[\frac{2x^{\frac{3}{2}}y^3}{\sqrt{z}}\right]^2$$

$$=\left[\frac{2x^{\frac{3}{2}}y^3}{z^{\frac{1}{2}}}\right]^2$$

$$=\frac{4x^3y^6}{z}$$

Question 26: C

In Y, the blood oxygen concentration significantly increases after passing the organ. This means that organ Y is the lungs. This narrows the options to A or C

In organ X, the salt, glucose and urea concentration in blood has decreased. We would not expect to see these changes in the heart – but in the kidney as a result of ultra-filtration.

Question 27: A

Drag will always be a positive value (you can't get negative air resistance!)

When the parachutist falls from the aircraft, drag will increase until they reach terminal velocity. When the parachute opens, drag will increase sharply to reduce the parachutist's velocity. As their velocity decreases, drag will decrease until the new terminal velocity is reached.

The air resistance at terminal velocity will be the same. Thus A is the correct answer.

Question 28: C

Since the compounds are all electrically neutral, the charges must balance:

A. $(+2) + (-3) + (-1) = -2$
B. $(+6) + (-6) + (-1) = -1$
C. $(+10) + (-9) + (-1) = 0$
D. $(+14) + (-10) + (-1) = +3$

Compound C is the only option which is electrically balanced.

Question 29: A

This question requires the use of the sine rule and is therefore no longer on the BMAT specification.

Using the sine rule:

$$\frac{PR}{Sin\ 45} = \frac{\sqrt{6}}{Sin\ 60}$$

$$PR = \frac{\sqrt{6}\ x\ Sin\ 45}{Sin\ 60}$$

$$Sin\ 45 = \frac{1}{\sqrt{2}},\ Sin\ 60 = \frac{\sqrt{3}}{2}$$

$$PR = \frac{\frac{\sqrt{6}}{\sqrt{2}}}{\frac{\sqrt{3}}{2}}$$

$$PR = \frac{2\sqrt{3}}{\sqrt{3}} = 2$$

END OF SECTION

Section 3

Explain what you think the author means by the term 'ethical market'.

➤ The article gives the following definition for an ethical market: "The market would be confined to a self governing geopolitical area—for example, the UK or Australia. Vendors could sell into the system, from which their family members would stand a chance of benefiting. Only citizens from that area could sell and receive organs. There would be only one purchaser, an agency like the National Health Service (NHS) or Medicare, which would buy all organs and distribute according to some fair conception of medical priority. There would be no direct sales or purchases, no exploitation of low income countries and their populations."

➤ If the sale of organs became commonplace, a black market may rise. We do not know how each individual will respond to the removal of the organ and sale of organs may lead to manipulation of certain people in society.

➤ The author does make a good argument for the legalisation of organs - there is a huge transplant problem and this would provide motivation for more to donate. Furthermore, there is the consideration of patient autonomy, and the money obtained may be worth more than the lost organ.

A little learning is a dangerous thing (Alexander Pope)

➤ Alexander Pope suggests that learning is dangerous when it is incomplete. He implies that it is safer to know nothing, than to know a little and form the misconception that you are an expert on the subject.

➤ Suggest some examples of when a little learning may be a dangerous thing. Examples include a first year medical student wanting to perform an operation after reading about it; a pilot wanting to take-off after doing a flight simulation; self-diagnosis on the internet after reading a little about an illness; etc.

➤ However, it is unrealistic to expect everyone to either know everything or nothing about a subject and sometimes it is still useful to know a little about a subject. Examples: basic first aid or CPR knowledge can save a life; knowing the signs of stroke (even if you don't know what it actually is); understanding the symptoms of someone with a disease or mental illness so you can assist them and understand their behaviour; etc

➤ Whether a little learning is dangerous or not depends on the particular scenario. Usually it is useful in day-to-day life and is safe. However, in order to ensure it is not dangerous in, for example, medical cases, one must acknowledge their own limitations and ensure they know that they are not experts on a subject despite some low-level learning.

It is ridiculous to treat the living body as a mechanism.

➢   The statement suggests that it is a gross generalisation to regard the body as purely a succession of mechanisms.

➢   The 11 physiological systems within the body can often be considered mechanistically for doctors. The systems operate in a largely similar way for everyone and thus students can learn about each system in a general manner, and thus the pathology and pharmacology associated with each. (Give a more specific example)

➢   However, humans are all individual with distinct features and personalities and we must be treated as such. The experience of the same disease by different people is always unique. Some phenomena such as cognition and emotion cannot yet be explained mechanistically.

➢   We should not disregard considering the body mechanistically but we should also not only look at the body in this way.

➢   Ultimately, the body is a complex, coordinated collection of a vast number of mechanisms, some of which we do not yet understand, instead of being one ordinary, single mechanism that can be generalised for all.

Our belief in any particular natural law cannot have a safer basis than our unsuccessful critical attempts to refute it.

➢   Popper argues that the best way to support a theory is to refute false hypotheses, and that this offers more substantiation than directly finding positive evidence supporting a theory. Indeed, if we cannot find evidence disproving a theory, this suggests that it is more likely to be true.

➢   However, scientists do often aim to prove a law by attempting to provide evidence for it, as opposed to evidence against it, and this arguably a better method. Falsification alone does not necessarily identify the truthfulness of a proposition.

➢   Give an example - any scientific experiment where the result was determined directly, rather than through falsification.

➢   The key point here is probably that it is vital for a hypothesis to be testable so that we can develop evidence to whether it is correct, whether this occurs through lack of falsification or otherwise.

END OF PAPER

2004

Section 1

Question 1: C

A can be made by halving diagonally and then halving each of these, as can B. D can be made by splitting the 2 triangles on the end, and making the quadrilateral in the middle with 2 equivalent triangles. E can be split into the triangle at the top and the quadrilateral at the bottom, each made with 2 triangles. If in doubt, try making what you think the right-angled triangle may be and see if that can be used to make a table. The ends of C (the 2 triangles) cannot be used to make the middle quadrilateral.

Question 2: C

The conclusion of the argument is that by taxing something, which is dangerous to health, we can improve the health of the population. An example of this working is given by C. A, D and E are unrelated to this conclusion. B may be true but would not strengthen this particular argument.

Question 3: B

We are looking for the smallest number of screws. So to minimise our final answer, we can say that all 40 slot-headed screws are 3mm diameter, making 30 cross-headed screws 3mm diameter. Of these 30 cross-headed screws, to minimise our answer, we can assume 20 of them are NOT 50mm long (i.e. 35 or 20mm long), leaving 10 that are cross-headed, 3mm diameter and 50mm long.

Question 4: A

The flaw of this argument is a BMAT favourite - the fact that a correlation between 2 factors doesn't necessarily mean causation between them. They may be linked by another factor, or the causality may be in the opposite direction to that stated. Thus the assumption made in the conclusion, that whole class teaching being more beneficial, cannot necessarily be assumed without more information. B is irrelevant, C is not necessarily assumed and D and E may not be true.

Question 5: C

Tom takes 15 minutes less than Suki as he leaves 10 minutes later and arrives 5 minutes earlier, which is 0.25 hours. We know Tom's speed is 4v, so we can set up simultaneous equations using distance = speed x time.
$2 = 4v \times (t-0.25)$
$2 = vt$

Solve these simultaneous equations to get $t = 1/3$ hours. They meet when $t=1/3$ hours and $v = 6$km/h, and the distance at this time is 1km.

Question 6: E

The argument suggests that 'everyone who can own a pet, should do so' and this is because these people live longer. However, this assumes that everyone should try and live longer, which is said in E.

A is not necessarily assumed - this idea is a suggestion, and saying people with allergies CAN NEVER have pets is too strong.
B is not correct as the notion of multiple pets is not mentioned.
C is not necessarily assumed - 'the emotional benefits of affectionate relationships' isn't linked to particular animals.
D is not necessarily an assumption.

Question 7: D

They share the profits equally, so £390 each for the work, so Bill owes Alf £390 here. Alf paid £240 for the materials, so Bill owes him half of this, so Bill owes Alf £120 for this. £390 + £120 is £510.

Question 8: 12.0, 12.5 or 13.0

Add up the episodes of care for each department as shown in the graph. (Roughly) 1.2 + 0.1 + 1.4 + 0.3 + 0.8 +1.4 +0.8 +1.2 + 0.8 + 5 = 13.

Question 9: A

There are around 4.34 million days in hospital for cancer, and 1.4 million episodes. 4.34/1.4 is closest to 3.1 days. If this is not immediately obvious, then try 1.4 million x 3 days which is 4.2 million days, close to the total number of days. 1.4 million x 4 days is 5.6 million days, which is not close.

Question 10: A

~1.4 million cases of cancer, 1/7 are lung cancer which is roughly 200,000 cases of lung cancer overall. Thus, the cases for men must be lower than this - A is the only feasible answer. 120,000 is indeed 50% more than 80,000.

Question 11: A & C

The average stay is half that for cancer, and that may indeed be because some cancer treatment requires a short stay (A), or because some circulatory treatment requires long stays (C). B is not relevant, because the number of episodes is weighted relative to the total number of days. D is no relevant, as death is not a factor in the average stay calculation.

Question 12: B & C

B can be correct - 6 correct answers and 6 no answers. C can also be correct - 7 correct answers, 3 incorrect answers and 2 no answers.
A cannot be correct - 3 correct answers would give 15 points, and then no more can be gained to make 18.
D cannot be correct - 8 correct answers gives 24 points, but only 4 questions are left and 6 points must be lot. Only a maximum of 1 can be lost for each go. E is incorrect for an analogous reason.

Question 13: B

The final sentence, 'without this protection the seas would freeze solid, from the bottom up; and life as we know it, which began in water, would not exist,' argues that we must have this unusual property of water to survive, thus it is a necessary condition for life. However, the passage does not suggest this structure alone allows us to survive, so the unusual property is not a sufficient condition for life.

Question 14: B

Visualisation. B cannot be correct because if the shape is folded in this way, the 2 dots for the '2' face would not be at different vertices.

Question 15: D

The conclusion is the final sentence, which his paraphrased by D (the animal Kingdom involves both animals and humans of course). The conclusion is not about the relative importance of animal and human rights (A), the argument suggests experiments are sometimes beneficial (B and C) and non-medical research is not part of the argument (E).

Question 16: A

David is given as the heaviest in all of them, so we can ignore comparisons with him. We know that Colin has lost more weight than the other 2. However, he started lighter than Barbara and lost more weight so he could not have finished heavier than her - thus A must be incorrect.

Question 17: A

The conclusion is at the start, and then the argument gives the evidence to support this. This is all effectively paraphrased by A, which is the best answer.

B is part of the evidence rather than the conclusion, C is not said in the passage, D is not as good as A in summarising the main conclusion and E is again evidence rather than the conclusion.

Question 18: C

0.1 x 0.1 x 0.1mm cube: volume of 0.001 mm^3 and SA of 0.06mm^2.
Big cube: volume of 1000mm^3 and SA of 600mm^2

Number of little cubes = $1000/0.001 = 10^6$ cubes.
SA of all the little cubes: 10^6 x $0.06 = 6$ x 10^4 mm^2
SA of all the little cubes - big cube = $60000 - 600 = 59400$mm$^2 = 594$cm^2

Question 19: D

D is the only one that can be drawn from the passage without being inferred - associated is not too strong a word and the passage clearly suggests than lifelong exercise and good health are linked. All the others can only be inferred with assumptions.

Question 20: D

Max recommended daily intake is 6 grams per day. We know 15% of 567 men have had 6 grams or under. 567 x $0.15 = ~85$.

Question 21: 7.6

$66-31 = 35\%$ have between 6 and 9 grams. Assuming linearity, $19/35$ have between 6 and the median. 3 x $19/35$ is roughly 1.6, and $6 + 1.6 = 7.6$.

Question 22: A

To work out the estimated salt intake in intervals (e.g. 9-12 and 12-15) look at the value for the larger number in the interval and take away the smaller number in the interval (e.g. 15 and under - 12 and under to work out 12-15). Thus, A is the correct graph.

Question 23: B

If this calculation were done the assumption is that the values in the survey are evenly distributed across the age range, which is not necessarily true. The other answers would not cause bias.

Question 24: 10

18 patients taking 5 mins each = 90 mins. 1 patient takes 7 minutes longer, so 97 minutes. Emergency call of 8 mins makes 105, and emergency surgery of 5 mins makes 110. 2 hours is 120 minutes, so 120-110 = 10 minutes late.

Question 25: B

The conclusion is that the habitats of wading birds will inevitably decline, and this is due to peat. However, the assumption is that people will carry on using peat despite the alternatives. A, C, D and E are not necessarily assumed.

Question 26: A

There is no straightforward mathematical method to use here, except a problem solving method. Try listing the 'off' times for the 2 lights.
Lighthouse 1: 3, 14, 25, 36, **47**, 58, 69,...
Lighthouse 2: 2, 11, 20, 29, 38, **47**, ...

Since the lights were in sync 15 seconds ago, they will next appear together in $47 - 15 = 32$ seconds

Question 27: B

Doubling the height and diameter will increase the SA fourfold and the volume eightfold. The mass is therefore 800 x 4 = 3.2kg.
The water in the first container has a mass of 15.6 - 0.8kg = 14.8kg. The second has a volume 8 times of the first - 14.8 x 8 = 118.4 kg. Add the mass of the water - 3.2 + 118.4 = 121.6kg

Question 28: C

1 is correct - 30% work, at least some of the time, in the commercial sector, which covers doctors working in both and the commercial sector alone. Thus, some doctors must work in the public service only.
2 is also correct - 70% work solely in the public sector, whereas 30% work in either both or just commercial.
3 cannot be deduced - we don't know how much time doctors spend at each service.

Question 29: E

30g/L x 0.2 L + 20g/L x 0.05 L = concentration of solution x 0.25 L
7 = concentration of solution x 0.25 L. Thus, conc = 28g/L

Question 30: B

Use distance = speed x time at different points. We can rule out A and D immediately because it is obvious from the first times on the flat that the cyclist will be at the lead at the beginning. After 1km the runner will have been travelling for 1/6 hours, which is 10 mins, and the cyclist for 1/30 hours, which is 2 mins, so the cyclist is 8 mins ahead. For the next 1.5km the runner will have been travelling for 3/8 hours, which is 22.5 mins, and the cyclist for 30 mins, so the runner makes up 7.5 mins here and is now 0.5 mins ahead at 2.5km, as seen in B only.

Question 31: A & C

Express each one as an inequality - $a \leq s$, $s < a$, $s \geq a$ and $a \geq s$. From this you can see A and C are equivalent. If this is not obvious to you, try considering whether Anne can be older than Susan, whether Anne and Susan can be the same age or whether Anne can be younger than Susan for each one.

Question 32: 14%

The last sentence tells us that collision deaths fell to 4200 from 4900 in this period. Thus the percentage decrease is 700/4900 x 100, which is 1/7. Hopefully you know this is near to 14%.

Question 33: B

The sentence 'by 1992 sprains and strains had risen to 83%, and all other injuries had fallen to 40 per cent' only makes sense if some of the claims for the former came hand in hand with claims for the latter. The others are not sufficient explanations.

Question 34: 22

Between 1980 and 1993 the claims per hundred rose by 33% to 29.3, so to find the BI claims in 1980 we must divide 29.3 by 1.33. 1.33 can be treated as 4/3 here, so we can change our sum to 29.3 x 3/4, which is 21.9, 22 to the nearest whole number.

Question 35: B and C

A doesn't offer an explanation at all, so is not correct. B identifies a possible reason for why more have made BI claims and C suggests a difference if people do not claim when there is no visible damage.

END OF SECTION

Section 2

Question 1: A

Remember that hearts are drawn as if we were looking at the patient, so the left hand side of the paper is the right hand side of the heart. Blood enters from the pulmonary vein (2) to the left aorta (3) to the left ventricle (4) and is ejected through the aorta (1). It then renters through the vena cava (7), to the right aorta (6) to the right ventricle (5) to the pulmonary artery (8). Thus, the correct sequence is given by option A.

Question 2: B

$Area = \frac{1}{2} x\ base\ x\ height = \frac{1}{2} x (2 - \sqrt{2})(4 + \sqrt{2})$

$= \frac{8 + 2\sqrt{2} - 4\sqrt{2} - 2}{2}$

$= \frac{6 - 2\sqrt{2}}{2} = 3 - \sqrt{2}$

Question 3: 3, 12, 3, 6

The quickest way to do these type of questions is via algebraic equations. If you're unfamiliar with this approach then see the chemistry chapter in *The Ultimate BMAT Guide.*

For Copper: $q = s$

For Hydrogen: $r = 12$

For Oxygen: $3r = 6s + 6 + 2t$.

Since r = 12, this simplifies to: $\mathbf{15 = 3s + t}$

For Nitrogen: $r = 2s + t$.

Since $r = 12$, this simplifies to: $\mathbf{2s + t = 12}$

Solve simultaneously: $t = 15 - 3s$

Therefore $2s + 15 - 3s = 12$

Thus, $s = q = 3$

Substituting back into: $t = 15 - 3(3) = 6$

Question 4: E

Remember that $Moment = force\ x\ perpendicular\ distance\ to\ pivot$

At all points the product of force and perpendicular distance to the pivot is equal.

$Moment\ exerted = 60N\ x\ (0.16 + 0.04) = 12\ Nm$
Therefore the moment at the piston is $12\ Nm$

Thus the force applied to the piston $= \frac{12}{0.04} = 300N$

Question 5: 0.32A

$Charge = Current\ x\ Time$

$2\ x\ 10^{18}$ Ions move towards the electrodes per second so:

$Current = 2\ x\ 1.6\ x\ 10^{-19}\ x\ 10^{18} = 0.32\ A$

Question 6: E

This is very straightforward. During expiration, the intercostal muscles and the diaphragm relax. This results in a decrease in the volume of the thorax, which increases the Intrathoracic pressure. This causes air to move outside via the mouth.

Question 7: E, B, A, C

i)   A giant molecular structure would not conduct electricity and would have high melting and boiling points, hence E.
ii) Metals conduct electricity when solid and molten, hence B.
iii) Ionic compounds only conduct electricity when molten, hence A.
iv) The melting point of C is -20 and the boiling point is 58 so it is a liquid in-between these temperatures.

Question 8: E

Round 79.31 → 80% to make your life easier! Thus, 20% of mass is due to oxygen.

$$Moles\ of\ W = \frac{80}{184} \approx 0.4$$

$$Moles\ of\ O: \frac{20}{16} \approx 1.25$$

Thus, the molar ratio is $0.4 \approx 1.25$

The closest ratio to this is 1:3 giving a formula of WO_3.

Question 9: 7.2m

The question heavily implies that you can assume that:

Kinetic Energy is fully transformed to Gravitational Potential Energy.

Therefore, $E_p = E_k$

This gives: $\frac{mv^2}{2} = mg\Delta h$

Therefore, $v^2 = 2g\Delta h$

$$\Delta h = \frac{v^2}{2g} = \frac{144}{20} = 7.2m$$

~ 43 ~

Question 10: A and B

This is no longer on the BMAT specification.

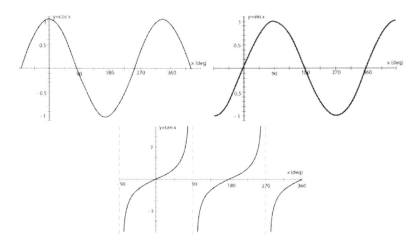

A. $\alpha + \theta = 180$. Alpha + theta = 180 so A is true.
B. Beta = 360 - theta so B is true.
C. Gamma and theta are the same as they are alternate angles, so C is false.
D. Sin 180 = 0 so D is false.

Question 11: B

Here, a ketone group (R-C=O) has been converted into an alcohol group (R-C-OH). The addition of hydrogen makes this a reduction reaction.

Question 12: D

The male carries a recessive allele on his X chromosome so this could only be passed on to his daughters - 4 and 5. If 4 had the allele, it could also be passed to either of her children - 8 or 9.

Question 13: D

Rearrange the equation: $x^2 + 2x - 8 \geq 0$

Factorise: $(x - 2)(x + 4) \geq 0$

Remember that this is a quadratic inequality so requires a quick sketch to ensure you don't make a silly mistake with which way the sign is.

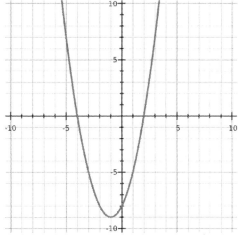

Thus, $y = 0$ when $x = 2$ and $x = -4$

$y > 0$ when $x > 2$ or $x < -4$

Thus, the solution is: $x \leq -4 \; and \; x \geq 2$

Question 14: D

Smaller molecules diffuse faster along the tube. The white ring is closer to the concentrated HCl so the ammonia molecule has diffused further, and thus the mass of ammonia molecules is less than the mass of HCl molecules.

~ 45 ~

Question 15: False, false, true, false, false

Closing S1 keeps the same voltage across the bulb and voltmeter which are all in parallel, and because of Ohms Law, I is therefore same too. Hence a and b are false.

Closing S2 will increase the current across A2 due to the decrease in total resistance as an alternative path is provided, but the V and hence I across A3 is the same as nothing is added in series, therefore the entire voltage is dropped across the bulb.

Closing S3 will short out the circuit therefore negligible current will flow through the ammeters and this is a huge decrease in reading to as near as makes no difference zero.

Question 16: B

Let P represent a health problem and N represent normal.

There are three permutations to choose one P and 2 x N: PNN, NPN, NNP

The overall probability $= 3 \, x \frac{1}{4} x \frac{3}{4} x \frac{3}{4} = \frac{27}{64}$

Question 17: D

Since $g = 10ms^{-2}$, the parachutist's weight $= 90 \, x \, 10 = 900N$

Since the parachutist is travelling at terminal velocity:

$Air \; resistance = Weight = 900N$

Question 18: D

In a hydrocarbon, a single hydrogen atom is replaced by NH_2. Thus, an amine has one more hydrogen atom and one more nitrogen atom than a hydrocarbon. Thus, D is correct.

Question 19: A, D and E

Remember that all gametes are haploid and have half the number of chromosomes of a normal body cell. Thus, C and F are abnormal.

Ova can only contain an X chromosome → B is abnormal.

Question 20: C

If you get stuck with these type of questions – write down every relevant equation e.g. $P = IV, V = IR, Q = It$ etc. This will make it easier to rearrange equations to get the correct units.

A. $P = IV$ and since $I = \frac{Q}{t}$, $P = \frac{Q}{t} x V$
B. From Ohm's Law, $V = IR, P = IV = I x IR = I^2 R$
C. There is no way to get these units to equal a Watt.
D. $P = IV$
E. From Ohm's Law, $I = \frac{V}{R}, P = IV = \frac{V}{R} x V = \frac{V^2}{R}$

Question 21: D

Unlike the other vessels, the hepatic portal vein carries nutrient rich blood from one organ to another (gut → liver). Contrastingly, the others only carry blood to/from one organ.

Question 22: F

In the first decay, the atomic number increases by 1 and the mass number stays the same. This is an example of Beta decay – when a neutron transforms into an electron and proton.

In the second decay, the atomic number decreases by 2. This is an example of alpha decay- when 2 protons and 2 neutrons are emitted. Thus, X decreases by 4: $A - 4$.

Question 23: E

Oxygen displaces water and carbon monoxide displaces oxygen, so the iron-water bond is the weakest, and iron-carbon monoxide bond is the strongest. Iron-Oxygen bond is between these two.

Question 24: C

This is no longer on the BMAT Syllabus however you might be able to deduce it based on the shape of legs.

The right knee joint has extended. This is brought upon by contraction of R and relaxation of the antagonistic P.

The right ankle joint has also extended. This is brought upon by contraction of T and relaxation of the antagonistic S.

Option C is the only answer that satisfies these.

Question 25: D

$$T = 2\pi\sqrt{\frac{k^2+h^2}{gh}}$$

$$\frac{T}{2\pi} = \sqrt{\frac{k^2+h^2}{gh}}$$

$$\left(\frac{T}{2\pi}\right)^2 = \frac{k^2+h^2}{gh}$$

$$\frac{T^2}{4\pi^2} = \frac{k^2+h^2}{gh}$$

$$k^2 + h^2 = \frac{T^2 gh}{4\pi^2}$$

$$k^2 = \frac{T^2 gh}{4\pi^2} - h^2$$

$$k = \sqrt{\frac{T^2 gh}{4\pi^2} - h^2}$$

Question 26: Mitosis, both, meiosis, meiosis, both

i)   Only mitosis produces clones.
ii) Both replicate all chromosomes prior to any division.
iii) Gametes are only produced by meiosis.
iv) Haploid nuclei are only produced by meiosis.
v)   Genetic material will always appear as distinct chromosomes.

Question 27: C

Consider $(x - a)(x - b) = 0$

This can be expanded to: $x^2 - (a + b)x + ab = 0$.

$a + b = 7$ and $ab = 9$. Substitute this into the equation to give:

$x^2 - 7x + 9 = 0$

END OF SECTION

Section 3

Individual freedom and the rule of law are mutually incompatible.

➢ The statement suggests that the laws in place are against personal freedom, and that the two cannot occur synonymously.

➢ There are a number of examples of issues facing modern society whereby complete freedom is denied due to legality. One example is freedom of expression, which is considered a political right, but is restricted in content (and varies hugely between different countries). Others include euthanasia and abortion after 24 weeks - patients do not have autonomy here because the law dictates that they cannot carry this out in the UK, and patients may go abroad instead.

➢ However, the converse argument is that these laws do indeed allow freedom (albeit to a limited extent). The fact that freedom of expression is considered a human right, or that abortion is allowed prior to 24 weeks, allows people to do what they want within reason. Furthermore, the ability to express one's opinion within the boundaries of the law has been effective in making changes in society - for example the suffragettes for women's rights, Martin Luther King against racism, etc. The advent of media such as the internet and worldwide satellite broadcasting has allowed the emergence of more opportunities for freedom.

➢ Freedom is essential in any democracy in order to allow the public to be involved in decisions. However, the limits ensure that hatred and offence is not spread which would ostracise certain groups from society (arguably the exact opposite of what free speech intends to do).

There is more to healing than the application of scientific knowledge.

➤ Scientific knowledge allows the explanation of events based on objective observation. A hypothesis is developed and is tested experimentally, ensuring many factors are controlled for. Studies are tested and peer reviewed before a theory is accepted and this knowledge can then be used to develop new treatments. Along with the application of science, it is important to consider the art of managing patients. More and more, doctors are encouraged to take more of a holistic approach to care and consider the social and psychological aspects of treatment too.

➤ Treatments not wholly based upon scientific knowledge could be inferior in both efficacy and safety. Without rigorous clinical testing, patients may be put at risks and the drug may not be as effective as one designed through rational consideration of biochemical and physiological pathways. Indeed, when certain alternative treatments have been critically analysed, such as homeopathy, it can be seen that there is almost no effect relative to placebo.

➤ Many treatments use a 'reverse engineering' approach whereby the exact mechanism or science of the technology is not known but a clear therapeutic benefit is seen. One example is Deep Brain Stimulation for Parkinson's Disease which is currently the most efficacious treatment available but its method of action is still up for debate. Although it is desirable to understand how this technique works in order to perfect the parameters, it is not vital to know as long as it is not detrimental to the patient in other ways. Furthermore, several studies have shown that patients who are more comfortable around their doctor are more likely to improve in health, and the placebo effect is a known example of successful healing with no obvious scientific basis.

~ 51 ~

Our genes evolved for a Stone Age life style. Therefore, we must adopt Stone Age habits if we are to be healthy.

➤ Hundreds of millions of years of evolution led to our human ancestors, the Homo erectus, becoming the highest animal on Earth with a highly developed brain and adaptations allowing survival and hunting. Since then, our genetic makeup has changed relatively little, but we have changed significantly in a short space of time. This statement argues that because natural selection generated these very particular set of genes on Earth, it must be that the environment where our genotype was selected is where we are likely to function optimally. However, the sentences are not necessarily logically connected and we may be able to live better without Stone Age habits despite having 'Stone Age genes'. (Also, see the concept of memes devised by Richard Dawkins, which act as cultural analogues of genes and allow changes in society that are much quicker than that which can be spread by genes.)

➤ IF we were to agree with the reasoning and implement Stone Age habits, one could argue for some benefits such as more exercise and less processed food. However, with over 7 billion humans in the world, it would be completely unrealistic to do this; for example, food demand would completely outstrip demand. Also, we would have to lose some of our greatest inventions to date and this would set back progress by thousands of years.

➤ The best conclusion would probably suggest that the statement is understandable but not viable or realistic.

END OF PAPER

2005

Section 1

Question 1: C

Count up the tiles - there are 9 black (large), 9 white (medium) and 20 grey (small) so the proportion needed is roughly 1:1:2.

Question 2: D

The conclusion is that "schools should revert to traditional sports days" and the evidence is that because "adult life [involves] competition." To link this evidence to the conclusion the assumption is that school sports should prepare children for adult life.
None of the others are assumptions that must be made, and A and B are not even relevant to the argument.

Question 3: B

Julia counted the animals - $b + s = 13$
Tim counted the legs (birds have 2, sheep have 4) - $2b + 4s = 36$
Solve the simultaneous equations (e.g. double the first one and then take it away from the second) and you should get $s = 5$ and $b = 8$.

Question 4: A

This answer gives a reason for how the universe may be expanding overall but why galaxies can still collide.
B is not correct as it is too specific - we want a reason why galaxies in general collide.
C is not correct because it does not explain why there are collisions.
D doesn't really explain anything, and E is irrelevant.

Question 5: 30 to 49

Look at the columns which show the same years for males and females. Only for the ages 30-34, 35-39, 40-44 and 45-49 do the cancer deaths for females exceed males in all years shown. We only need to check between 30-54 because we are told that in 1991-95, every other age has more male deaths. For 50-54, there were more male deaths in 1971-75 than female.

Question 6: B

The conclusion is that "since our consumption of natural pesticides vastly outweighs that of synthetic pesticides, our health is at greater risk from natural pesticides than from synthetic ones." So to weaken this we want a reason why this may not be true. B is the only one that provides this.
A and C actually support the argument, and D is not relevant for the comparison between natural and synthetic pesticides.

Question 7: £10,500

Stamp duty will be 3% looking at the graph, and 3% of £350000 is £10500 (try multiplying by 3 and dividing by 100).

Question 8: C

There must be almost vertical parts to the graph, as for a £1 increase between e.g. £119999 and £120000 there will be a huge increase in tax, so B is incorrect.
D is also incorrect, as the tax paid will not be constant within a band - it will be relative to how much your house is within the band.
Finally, C is correct and A isn't, as the not vertical parts of the graph will become steeper as the percentage tax paid increases for each band.

Question 9: B

First £120000 is free.
Next £130000 is taxed at 1% - £1300 to pay on this.
Next £50000, to get up to the total of £300000, is taxed at 3%, so £1500 to pay on this.
So £1300 + £1500 to pay = £2800

Question 10: £3300

Price without 'cheating' - £260000 x 3% = £7800 tax
Price with cheating - £250000 x 1% (we can round up the £1 as it is basically insignificant when finding a percentage) = £2500 tax. Add the £2000 extra paid to make this £4500 (the £10000 paid is not an extra, as this would be paid in the price without cheating anyway).
£7800 - £4500 = £3300.

Question 11: A

Use the Venn Diagram - from the information we know the small circle is Spanish, the circle on the left is French and the circle on the right is German. Thus, the shaded area represents those who do French and German but not Spanish.

Question 12: E

This answer is correct, as the argument suggests more children have started using cannabis before age 15 but the levels of schizophrenia have remained stable so that cannabis cannot cause schizophrenia. However, if E is true, then we would have to wait some time to see whether cannabis can cause schizophrenia.
A supports the argument, B is irrelevant as the argument is about schizophrenia (a mental illness) and not cancer (a physical illness), C is far too general and D is not directly relevant to the conclusion.

Question 13: B

The first ray of incident light must transmit through 2 layers, each with a probability of 0.8 of transmitting, so 0.8 x 0.8 = 0.64.

However, some of the light that is transmitted through the first sheet will then be reflected by the second sheet, which will then again be reflected by the first sheet, then finally transmitted by the second sheet. The probability of this is 0.8 x 0.15 x 0.15 x 0.8 = 0.0144. The light can, in theory, be reflected infinite times between the 2 layers before being transmitted to the inside room, but the likelihood of this will be minute.

So the probability is 0.64 + 0.0144 (as any further probabilities are too small to consider if we need an answer to the nearest 1%), and 65% is the closest to this.

Question 14: E

1 is correct as the conclusion is that 'nuclear power…will have to continue to be used in 2050' and the evidence is that energy consumption will reach the target and be very high at this point, but to link these we need the assumption that the energy consumption will actually be that high in 2050.

2 is irrelevant to the conclusion - whether we can store nuclear waste or not, the argument is that we must continue using this power.

3 is correct as the evidence suggests 'these [renewable] sources will be unable to meet the shortfall in supply,' which assumes the development of these energy sources will be constant.

Question 15: D

The shopkeeper buys 4 packets (4p), and sells them for the price of 3 packets (3y), and gains 20% profit. Thus, $3y/4p = 1.2$, which you can rearrange to get $y=1.6p$. Thus, usually, there is a 60% profit made.

Question 16: D

This is (hopefully) a quite simple, 'reading of the graph' question. When the dipstick measures 0.15m he has 400 litres of oil. If he orders 500 litres more, he has 900 litres of oil. If 900 litres are present the dipstick should read about 0.6m.

Question 17: E

The theme of the argument is that we cannot say that we are ruining the countryside's natural beauty only through wind farms, as many other factors have already caused the British countryside to change in appearance since the 12th century. Thus E is the best answer.

A is too general as the argument is specifically about the countryside.

B, C and D are irrelevant to the general theme of the argument.

Question 18: C

The argument suggests that "we should not tolerate aggressive behaviour in a civilised society" and goes on to say that players who do this should be "banned from the club's next three game." However, to link these ideas we need the assumption that the ban would help to reduce the aggressive behaviour, which is what C says.

The rest of the answers cannot be inferred/are not necessarily true and they are therefore not assumptions made.

Question 19: 3200 (3100 allowed)

The division annual rate before the installation of CCTV (the column with 'start') is 37838. We want a monthly rate, so we divide this by 12 to get just over 3150, which rounds up to 3200 (but don't worry too much about being exact as 3100 is also accepted).

Question 20: F

All of the statements are confounding factors. We have a negative correlation between CCTV installation in the target area and overall crime in the area but this may not be a causal link and the other answers give other reasons as to why this may have occurred.

Question 21: 9%

The target area % change is (131-161)/161 which is roughly -30/160, which is 18.75%. The division % change is (6442-7164)/7164 which is roughly -700/7000 which is 10%. The difference between these is roughly 9%.

Question 22: 22%

If we remove the vehicle crime figures from the overall crime figures, we have a start rate of 1526 - 279 = 1247 and an end rate of 1098 - 126 = 972. The new percentage change is (972-1247)/1247 = roughly -275/1250 = 22% change

Question 23: E

Re-read what the buffer area is - an area surrounding a target area. Providing data about this tells us if the target area crime has just relocated to an adjacent area, and it helps us to determine whether the CCTV has caused falling crime in the target area of if this is more of a general trend.
2 is not correct as it is irrelevant to the idea of a buffer area.

Question 24: A & C

There are too many students getting very high marks, suggesting that the hard questions are too easy. There are also not enough students getting low marks, suggesting that the easy questions are also too easy.

Question 25: C

The path plan shows between which letters you can travel without encountering any other letter.
C to X can only be reached via I, so is wrong.
A to I can only be reached via C, so is wrong.
E to G can be reached directly, so is right.
F to G can only be reached via E, so is wrong.
J to X can only be reached via I, so is wrong.

Question 26: A

The medullary bone is only found in the female birds. Thus, the absence of it is necessary to determine whether the fossil is male - if the bone is present there is no way that it is a male. However, it is not sufficient, because the passage continues to say that the medullary bone is depleted during certain times in the female, so the absence of it alone does not mean that it is a male.

Question 27: B

1 is correct. Even if the 30% representing the 17-34 year olds were responsible for all the walking/cycling (10%) and public transport use (15%), then 5% would still use a car, and 5/30 is 1/6.
2 is correct as 30% are 16 or under, but only 15% of the total travel by public transport. Even if this was made up of all those 16 or under, at least 15/30 = 50% or under would travel by other means.
3 is not necessarily correct - 85% are under 60, and with this data alone it could be the case that all of them travel by car and public transport, and none by walking/cycling.

Question 28: B

Firstly, find the groups of 4 that add up to 14. The first that is fully available is 4 4 2 4, next is 1 5 6 2, next is 4 2 5 3 and finally we have 5 5. The next 2 numbers must add up to 4, so 4 is not viable. If it were 1 or 3, there would have been 5 consecutive odd numbers, which is not possible. Thus, 2 is the only possible answer.

Question 29: F

The conclusion is 'global travel helps to immunise the population' based on the information given.
1 is correct because if many British residents do not travel, then based on the conclusion we still need to be concerned about bird flu.
2 is correct because even if we are immune to many diseases, it does not mean that 'there is no chance that bird flu will kill thousands of people' as we may not be resistant to this one.
3 is correct as the evidence suggests the quality of nutrition has improved due to having a strong economy, but nutrition is also dependent on e.g. environmental conditions, what chemicals are used, processing, etc.

Question 30: D

Method 1: Rank the best car as 1 and the worst as 4. There are 24 possible sequences of which order they come in: 1234, 1243, 1324, 1342, 1423, 1432, 2134, 2143, 2314, 2341, 2413, 2431, 3124, 3142, 3214, 3241, 3412, 3421, 4123, 4132, 4213, 4231, 4312, 4321. 11 of these events (2134, 2143, 2314, 2341, 2413, 2431, 3124, 3142, 3412, 4123, 4132) result in him getting the best car.

Method 2: Work out that if 1 is the first, the probability of getting the best car is 0. If 2 is first, the probability of getting the best car is 1. If 3 is first, the probability of getting the best car is 1/2 (could have picked 2) and if 4 is first, the probability of getting the best car is 1/3 (could have picked 2 or 3). Add these together and divide by 4 (as each option has a ¼ chance of occurring) to get 11/24.

Question 31: A

As the paragraph discusses risks and benefits of aspirin, we can conclude that 1 is correct.
2 is wrong - 'certainly' is too bold a phrase and we don't know what the risk is for each individual patient.
3 is wrong and nothing like this is included in the passage.

Question 32: D

Deduce what the sequence is based on the information given. Hopefully you should see that the symbols represent $(2 \times 5 \times 5 \times 5) + (3 \times 5) + 1 = 250 + 15 + 1 = 266$.

Question 33: B

1 in 3 had visited an alternative therapist out of a total of 247 million patients, and 247/3 is roughly 82 million visiting alternative therapists. 425 million visits were made to alternative health practitioners, so per patient this is $425/82 = 5$

Question 34: C

The passage talks about how 'the time it takes is…at a premium…this is the void that alternative medicine appears to be filling.' Thus, this suggests that C is correct.
Although we know that time is at a premium, A is not necessarily true. B is not necessarily true - the author talks about different definitions of 'alternative medicine' and some may claim to cure individual diseases. D is not true - although it says 'the cornerstone of alternative medicine appears to be the belief in the body's ability to heal itself' this is not necessarily saying that doctors don't believe the same. It is too bold a statement.
E is not necessarily true for a similar reason to B - some treatments may have side effects and this does not necessarily mean it scores over conventional medicine anyway.

Question 35: D

This is true as the passage suggests that doctors having less time for patients has meant the 'void' is filled by alternative medicine.

A is not implied - even if they now have 'side-effects' this does not mean that the disease has not been cured

B is not correct - we know the 'best doctors are frustrated that combining the art of healing…is more difficult to do' but this does not mean they support alternative techniques.

C cannot be implied - there is nothing about pharm companies.

END OF SECTION

Section 2

Question 1: A

This is no longer on the BMAT syllabus.

Tidal volume is the volume of air displaced during normal ventilation in the absence of extra respiratory effort i.e. the normal volume of air that you breathe in & out.

Question 2: B

A burning splint makes:

➤ A popping sound if hydrogen is present
➤ goes out if carbon dioxide present
➤ A glowing splint relights if oxygen is present

➤ Bromine water is to test for C=C bonds
➤ Limewater is turned cloudy by carbon dioxide
➤ Litmus paper tests for pH but this is not useful for gasses.

Question 3: D

The number of protons has stayed the same (atomic number: 54+38=92) but the atomic mass has decreased by 4 (95+139=234). Thus, four neutrons must have been emitted in addition to the main products.

Question 4: C

Current will take the path of least resistance. Thus, for current to flow through the ammeter, it must follow the path:

R → Ammeter → Q or P → Ammeter → S

Since two resistors have lower resistances, current will 'prefer' to flow through them.

A. The resistance of p and q is lower so all current would travel through the top branch.
B. The resistance of p and r is lower so the current would remain split equally between the branches and carry on in the same branch.
C. The resistance of r and q is lower so the current will travel from r to q via the ammeter.
D. The resistance of r and s is lower so all current would travel through the bottom branch only.

Question 5: A

This is no longer on the BMAT Syllabus.

Smoking results in the production of carbon monoxide which irreversibly binds to haemoglobin, preventing it from binding to oxygen. This reduces the overall oxygen carrying capacity of red blood cells.

Question 6: C

$z = xy^2$

$1.2 \times 10^{13} = 3 \times 10^{-6}y^2$

$y^2 = \frac{1.2 \times 10^{13}}{3 \times 10^{-6}}$

$y^2 = 0.4 \times 10^{19} = 4 \times 10^{18}$

$y = 2 \times 10^9$

Question 7: A

Since a molecule is being broken down, this is a type of decomposition reaction (not synthesis).

Since there were 12 hydrogen atoms initially and only 8 in the products, 4 hydrogen atoms have been lost. Therefore, this is also an oxidation reaction.

Question 8: A

If the allele for long lashes was recessive, B and D would also have long lashes. Thus, the long lashes allele must be dominant. Thus, A must be heterozygous for the allele. C and E could be heterozygous but they could also be homozygous. B and D have short lashes so are homozygous recessive.

Question 9: C

$$A \propto \frac{1}{B^2}$$

Thus, if B is increased by 40%, then:

$$A \propto \frac{1}{(1.4B)^2}$$

$$A \propto \frac{1}{1.96B^2}$$

$$A \propto \frac{100}{196B^2} = \frac{25}{49B^2}$$

A is thus $\frac{25}{49}$ of what it was before, which is just over 50%. Thus, the decrease in percentage terms must be just under 50%, so a 49% decrease is the best answer.

Question 10: 39 cm

The bar is in equilibrium so: Moments clockwise = moments anti-clockwise

The bar exerts its weight at its centre of gravity which is 15 cm left of the pivot.

Therefore: $0.1 \times 800 = 200x + 10 \times 0.15$

$80 = 200x + 1.5$

$78.5 = 200x$

$x = \frac{78.5}{200} = 0.3925 \, m$

$= 39 \, cm$

Question 11: D

This question is no longer on the BMAT specification   .
The formula for sodium carbonate is Na_2CO_3 and since it is a 'decahydrate', it contains $10 \times H_2O$ molecules as well. Thus:

$$Fraction = \frac{Mass\ of\ Water}{Mass\ of\ Sodium\ Carbonate\ Dehydrate}$$

$$Fraction = \frac{10\,(16+1+1)}{23x2+12+3x16+10\,x\,(16+1+1)}$$

$$= \frac{18\,x\,10}{46+12+48+180}$$

Question 12: B

This is no longer on the BMAT specification.
When you look into the distance, the suspensory ligaments tighten to make the lens less convex so that you can cover more area, and the ciliary muscles relax.

Question 13: A

$$y = \left[\frac{x^2+2ax}{b}\right]^{\frac{1}{2}}$$

$$y^2 = \frac{x^2+2ax}{b}$$

$$by^2 = x^2 + 2ax$$

Complete the square to give: $by^2 = (x + a)(x + a) - a^2$

$$by^2 + a^2 = (x + a)^2$$

$$x + a = (by^2 + a^2)^{\frac{1}{2}}$$

$$x = (by^2 + a^2)^{\frac{1}{2}} - a$$

Question 14: B

$$Distance\ travelled = Transmitter\ to\ foetus\ +\ foetus\ to\ receiver$$

$$= 0.1 + 0.1 = 0.2m$$

$$Time = \frac{distance}{speed}$$

$$= \frac{0.2}{500} = 0.0004s$$

$$= 0.4\ ms$$

Question 15: D

The products consist of 6 x N − H bonds (= 6z)

The reactants consist of 1 x N≡N (= x) and 3 x H − H bonds (= 3y).

The reaction is exothermic so:

$$\sum Bond\ strength\ of\ Products > \sum Bond\ strength\ of\ Reactants$$

Thus, 6z > x + 3y

Question 16: D, C then G

This is no longer on the syllabus but you can work it out if you understand basic anatomy.

➤ A is bone
➤ B is a muscle that causes flexion at the <u>proximal</u> hinge joint when it contracts.
➤ C connects two bones together like a ligament.
➤ D is the end of the muscle body of B and inserts into the bone, similar to a tendon.
➤ E is a muscle body that causes extension at the <u>distal</u> hinge joint when it contracts.
➤ F is a muscle body that causes flexion at the <u>distal</u> hinge joint when it contracts.
➤ G is a muscle that causes extension at the <u>proximal</u> hinge joint when it contracts.
➤ E and F are antagonistic to each other; B and G are also antagonistic to each other.

~ 68 ~

Question 17: A

$$\left(\sqrt{5} - \sqrt{2}\right)^2 \left(\sqrt{5} + \sqrt{2}\right)^2$$

$$\left(5 - 2\sqrt{2}\sqrt{5} + 2\right)\left(5 + 2\sqrt{2}\sqrt{5} + 2\right)$$

$$\left(7 - 2\sqrt{10}\right)\left(7 + 2\sqrt{10}\right)$$

$$49 - 14\sqrt{10} + 14\sqrt{10} + 4(10)$$

$$49 - 40 = 9$$

Question 18: B

The maximum possible age of the rock would be if it consisted entirely of ^{235}U at the start. Since there are 8 parts in total:

Number of Half Lives	Proportion of ^{235}U	Proportion of ^{207}Pb
0	8	0
1	4	4
2	2	6
3	1	7
4	0.5	7.5

After 3 half lives, the rock would contain one part U^{235} to seven parts of Pb^{207}. Thus, the maximum age:

$$= 3 \times 7.1 \times 10^8 = 21.3 \times 10^8 \, years$$

$$= 2.13 \times 10^9 \, years$$

Question 19: B

Using $n = cV$:

The number of moles of NaOH = $2 \times 50 \times 10^{-3} = 100 \times 10^{-3}$

$= 0.1 \, moles$

Since the molar ratio between NaOH and H_2X is 2:1, there are 0.05 moles of H_2X.

The M_r of the acid $= \frac{mass}{moles} = \frac{4.5}{0.05} = 90$

Question 20: C

Active transport requires ATP which is produced during aerobic respiration. This requires oxygen. In options A, B and D, the substance moves from a higher concentration to a lower concentration and can therefore occur via diffusion. Contrastingly, in option C, magnesium ions move from a lower concentration to a higher concentration. This is an example of active transport and therefore requires oxygen.

Question 21: A

The triangle is equilateral so AC = x

Thus, the radius of the circle $= \frac{x}{2}$

Area of the Semi-circle $= \frac{\pi}{2}r^2 = \frac{\pi}{2}(\frac{x}{2})^2 = \frac{\pi x^2}{8}$

Split triangle ABC into 2 x right angled triangles:

Using Pythagoras: $AB^2 = BD^2 + AD^2$

$BD^2 = x^2 - \left(\frac{x}{2}\right)^2$

$BD^2 = \frac{3x^2}{4}$

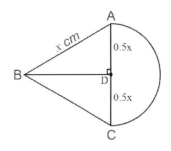

$$BD = \frac{\sqrt{3x^2}}{\sqrt{4}} = \frac{x\sqrt{3}}{2}$$

$Area\ of\ Triangle\ ABC\ =\ 2\ x\ Area\ of\ AD$

$$= 2\ x\frac{1}{2}\ x\frac{x}{2}\ x\ \frac{x\sqrt{3}}{2}$$

$$= \frac{x^2\sqrt{3}}{4}$$

$$Total\ Area = \frac{x^2\sqrt{3}}{4} + \frac{\pi x^2}{8}$$

$$= \frac{2x^2\sqrt{3} + \pi x^2}{8}$$

$$= \frac{x^2(2\sqrt{3}+\pi)}{8}$$

Question 22: D

Since g is not given, you can safely assume that $g\ =\ 10\ ms^{-2}$

Thus, g on the new planet $= \frac{1}{4}\ x\ 10\ =\ 2.5\ ms^{-2}$

$E_p\ =\ mg\Delta h\ =\ 1\ x\ 2.5\ x\ 20\ =\ 50J$

When the mass is dropped from the building, all of its gravitational potential energy is converted to kinetic energy, i.e. $E_p\ =\ E_k$

$E_k\ =\ \frac{mv^2}{2}$

$50\ =\ \frac{v^2}{2}$

$100\ =\ v^2$

$v\ =\ 10\ m/s$

Question 23: B

Let x be the number of hydrogen atoms and y be the number of Deuterium atoms.

The mass of 4 carbon atoms = 4 x 12 = 48

This contributes 80% to the compound so the other 20% is made up of hydrogen and deuterium.

I.e. H + D = 12

Since deuterium has a mass of 2, this can be represented as $x + 2y = 12$

There are 4 carbon atoms and $x + y = 10$ (because butane has 10 hydrogens).

Now we just solve the equations simultaneously: $x = 10 - y$

Substituting into the first equation gives: $10 - y + 2y = 12$

Thus, $y = 2$, $x = 8$

Therefore, the formula is $C_4H_8D_2$.

Question 24: A

This is actually a complex question. Firstly note that:

➤ Heart rate and stroke volume would be unaffected by the opening.
➤ The opening would also have no effect on the pulmonary vein (which normally carries oxygenated blood back to the left atrium).

This leaves us with options A and E.

Blood could flow:

1) Left atrium → Right atrium:

This would result in more blood being pumped to the lungs. However, this is unlikely to cause problems to the health of the baby.

2) Right atrium → Left atrium:

This would result in some deoxygenated being pumped by the left ventricle into the aorta. This would cause the baby to become hypoxic which is a major problem.

Question 25: B

$760\ mmHg\ =\ 100{,}000\ Pa = 10^5 Pa$

Thus, $Pressure\ = \frac{152}{760}\ x\ 10^5\ =\ 0.2\ x\ 10^5 Pa$

$2\ x\ 10^4 Pa$

$Area\ =\ 2cm^2\ =\ 2\ x\ 10^{-4}\ m^2$

$Force\ =\ Pressure\ x\ Area$
$Force\ =\ 2\ x\ 10^4\ x\ 2\ x\ 10^{-4}\ =\ 4N$

Question 26: D

These types of questions frequently come up so it's essential you know the reactivity series off by heart. From the given elements, Na is the most reactive and therefore, is hardest to displace from its oxide. Thus reaction D would require the highest temperature.

Question 27: 0.8

When you get a question like this, start off by drawing the diagram and filling in all of the information that you know:

Since D is opposite B, BD is also a diameter of the circle.

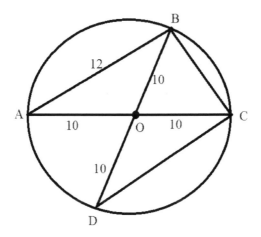

Since the angle in a semicircle is always 90°, ABC = 90 °

Therefore, ABC is a right angled triangle. Using Pythagoras:

$AB^2 + BC^2 = AC^2$

$BC^2 = 20^2 - 12^2$

$BC^2 = 400 - 144 = 256$

$Thus, BC = 16$

Note that BDC is also a right angled triangle. Thus:

$Sine\ BDC = \frac{BC}{BD} = \frac{16}{20} = 0.8$

END OF SECTION

Section 3

Animals do not feel pain as we do.

➢ This statement is probably not refuting the idea that animals can endure the same physical hurt and discomfort experienced by a noxious stimulus, which act on nociceptors common to almost all animal species. Instead, it is likely suggesting that they do not experience 'emotional suffering' in the same way.

➢ We cannot directly experience anyone else's pain; it is a state of consciousness. Thus, it is unlikely that we can ever answer this question unless we can get inside the head of an animal and actually be it. However, many scientists argue that the majority of animals (with the exception of primates, dolphins and some other higher mammals) are not conscious and thus do not have the same subjective experience of pain.

➢ Furthermore, only primates and humans have a neocortex - the 'thinking area' of the cortex, and this may be why we are able to feel pain without any physical damage.

➢ However, a capacity to feel emotional pain obviously enhances a species' prospects for survival, since it causes members of the species to avoid sources of injury. It is surely unreasonable to suppose that nervous systems that are virtually identical physiologically, have a common origin and a common evolutionary function, and result in similar forms of behaviour in similar circumstances should actually operate in an entirely different manner on the level of subjective feelings.

➢ Behavioural changes are similar during pain; for example, many animals display behaviours associated with depression during a painful experience such as lack of motivation and lethargy.

Science should leave off making pronouncements: the river of knowledge has too often turned back on itself.

➢ A scientific pronouncement is an authoritative declaration about findings that have been made. However, this statement suggests that we should be wary to make such announcements, as the findings made can later be found to be false.

➢ Andrew Wakefield is the gentlemen who asserted the link between the MMR vaccine and the onset of autism, which resulted in the deaths of many children from measles, mumps and rubella. AW falsified his results and subjected autistic subjects to unethical procedures to prove that the MMR vaccine cause autism after being bribed by a law firm that was planning on suing the MMR vaccine company. After repeat experiments were performed and the results acquired were found to be completely different, AW's paper was withdrawn from the Lancet and he was struck off the medical register. Sadly, the myth that MMR vaccines cause autism is still believed and herd immunity has not reached pre-scare levels, highlighting the danger of making such pronouncements.

➢ However, if pronouncements must be made to advance science then this is undoubtedly a positive. Indeed, passion, drive and intrigue are intrinsic to scientific discovery and enquiry; without these qualities, Fleming and Darwin may never have discovered antibiotics and evolution respectively. Without these pronouncements, it is unlikely that technological advances that were unplanned/unprecedented could be implemented.

➢ Furthermore, making pronouncements welcomes other scientists with different prejudices and preferences to follow what we have done to see if they get the same results through peer review, which furthers the reliability of all experiments.

~ 76 ~

With limited resources and increasing demand, doctors will not in the future be concerned about how to cure, so much as whether to cure.

➢   As the world population is growing exponentially and resources are become scarce, it is may be the case that in the future we will not be able to match the demand for medicine with supply. Then, we must then focus on how to best use the remaining resources, which will take importance over developing new treatments.

➢   Limited resources and increasing demand is likely, on a more global scale, due to the birth rate exceeding the death rate, causing overpopulation and famine. In this country, the issue is the ageing population.

➢   Thus, we may have to specifically provision and allocate specialist treatments to certain people only, if we are unable to provide them for everyone. Ethical and moral issues must be considered with each patient considered individually. Ultimately, refusing treatment to someone who will die without it, even if it is because someone 'deserves' or 'needs' it more, can be considered as passive euthanasia.

➢   The argument against this is that 'the care of the patient is your primary concern' and you 'should always act in the patients best interests,' ensuring the best quality of care possible. Withholding a treatment is certainly not fulfilling this in some instances.

➢   The whole principle of the NHS is equality of healthcare, and that is why it is often considered the 'crown jewel of the welfare state.' If we begin to tell people that they cannot have certain treatments then we are opposing the very principle of having a public healthcare system.

➢   What is the viability of the latter? The authorities can prioritise ensuring cost-effectiveness within medicine and equal consideration of all patients to try and match the supply and demand of resources and remove the concern of 'whether to cure', but achieving these is not necessarily feasible.

END OF PAPER

2006

Section 1

Question 1: C

Proportion of seabirds is 80, which decreased by 60%, so $0.4x = 80$ and $x = 200$.
Proportion of humans is 1, which increased by 25%, so $1.25y = 1$ and $y = 0.8$.
200: 0.8 → 250:1

Question 2: E

The conclusion is the last line, given away by the word 'so'. It states that 'freedom of speech...has to have limits put upon it if democracy is to be sustained.' This is clearly paraphrased in E, which is the correct answer.

Question 3: B

A 'worked solution' isn't really possible here, but it is not against the BMAT rules to bring scissors to the exam, so cut out the table and test which shapes are possible (provided you don't need the page before anymore!) 1 and 3 are possible and 2 and 4 are not. In the incorrect 2, both have inward facing lines to the middle which would not happen with these shapes. Also, as 2 and 4 are extremely similar (basically rotations of each other), you should deduce that if one is right the other probably is right, and vice versa.

Question 4: C

The conclusion is that 'political journalists are not doing their job properly' and the supporting evidence is that 'they exclude...political issues.' Thus, the unstated assumption to link this evidence to the conclusion is that it is the job of the political journalists to inform voters about the political issues. The conclusion still holds without A, B, D or E being assumed.

Question 5: 62 seconds

The second train will clearly take longer - it must travel the distance it is from the tunnel, the length of the tunnel for the front of the train to be at the end and the length of the train for the back of the train to be out of the tunnel.

$d = 40 + 615 + 120 = 775m$. The speed is always 45km/h so $t = 775/45000$. Through short division of $775/45$ ($=17.2$) you can work out that this is 0.0172 hours, which you can multiply by 3600 to give 62 seconds.

Question 6: C

The phrases 'on the one hand' and 'on the other hand' and giving 2 separate examples of how the media approaches the issue of eating disorders highlights the inconsistency, so C is the correct answer.

A cannot be deduced - we do not know what they are MORE influenced by.

B cannot be inferred - we do not know if they are aware or unaware of the effects.

D is too bold - we do not know if they are ONLY interested in thin fashion models.

E is not relevant here - it is not related to how the print media approach the issue of eating disorders.

Question 7: B

If we look at the 'Total' row at the bottom, and compare GCSE performance (the initial information suggests this is done by determining how many had 5 or more GCSE passes at A* to C), Asian pupils have 58.7% and white students have 55.1%. $58.7 - 55.1 = 3.6\%$, so this is 4% when rounded.

Question 8: E

The column we are looking at is the 'KS 2-4 VA Measure' for students 'other than English as a first language.' The highest value in this column when looking at boys and girls combined is for the Chinese students.

Question 9: D

This is correct - if we look at % with 5A*-C for both boys and girls, and compare those who either have English as their first language or don't, we can see that only Mixed students perform better at GCSE than their equivalents.

A is not correct - Boys (977.5) have a lower value of total KS 2-4 VA Measure than Girls (997.3).

B is not correct - more Asian students (~30000/35000) have English as a second language then Chinese pupils (~1750/2250).

C is not correct - the difference between white girls and white boys is 60.2 - 50.3 = 9.9, but this difference is smaller for Chinese pupils (85.1 - 77.1 = 8).

Question 10: D

A B and C are possible reasons. This effect occurs for all ethnic groups, and the fact that there is a bigger difference in improvement for Asian girls than Asian boys is irrelevant. For example, even if we removed all the values for Asians, it would still be true that 'for all ethnic groups, girls improve more between the ages 11 and 16 than boys.'

Question 11: E

Here we have a negative correlation between cannabis use and ability to recall words. This could be due to any of the reasons given. 1 and 2 highlights that cannabis itself could be the causal factor whereas 3 highlights that it could also be because there is a difference in IQ between the groups, independent of cannabis use.

Question 12: A

At $1.50, the supplier gets 90c (60%) and the store gets 60c. With the offer, 1 box of cereal costs $1, so the supplier gets 60c and the store gets 40c.

The supplier must reduce the price by 90c - 60c = 30c.

Question 13: 68p

We must go through the postal rates from cheapest to most expensive and see the first value we get that we cannot be made using only 1 or 2 stamps.

23p - 1 23p stamp
32p - 1 32p stamp
37p - 1 37p stamp
49p - 1 49p stamp
50p - 1 50p stamp
62p - 1 42p stamp and 1 20p stamp
68p - cannot be made with 1 or 2 stamps, so this is our answer.

Question 14: C

The conclusion is that 'experts...agree that it is a completely reliable method of identifying criminals.' However, as C says, this is an opinion and not necessarily fact, which is the weakness of the argument. A is tempting but is not the best answer because it is too general and the argument is not about how they **apply** their method. B basically paraphrases the first line of the argument, and this is then countered within the argument, so it is not really a weakness.
D is not a weakness as it is already stated in the argument and the argument is that the technique is reliable because of the opinion of experts rather than about how long it has been used for.

Question 15: C

Remember that 'Due' means directly when thinking about directions. So if Wellbank is due east of Ruilick, and Aultviach is due north of Ruilick, Ruilick must be E (as it is the only one with something directly North and directly East of it), Wellbank must be F and Aultviach must be A. Then, if Rheindown is due south of Clashandarran then Rheindown is D and Clashandarran is C. This leaves C and G. If Beauly is south and west of Windyhill then Beauly must be G and Windyhill is C.

Question 16: B

1 is not an assumption - we do not know if less developed countries have set targets or not.

2 is not an assumption – there is no mention of whether developed countries are prioritising global warming or current poverty.

3 is not an assumption - we don't know if levels of prosperity are changing.

4 is an assumption - the argument suggests that there is a choice between either reducing poverty or decreasing greenhouse emissions.

Question 17: B

10 children overall, spending £125 - 10 x 25p (as they all get a 25p packet of bubble gum) = £122.50 spent.

2 went on the Apocalypse and the Carousel - 2 x (9 + 3.50) = £25, leaving £97.50 spent on the other 8 children.

If x went on Armageddon and dodgems and y went on Armageddon and helter skelter, $12.5x + 12y = 97.5$, and $x + y = 8$. You could either solve this, or quickly test each number given in the answer, and you should get $x = 3$.

Question 18: C

The conclusion is 'people do not have the right to complain about farmers' use of pesticides' and the evidence given is that they would 'make a loss' otherwise. The assumption made linking this evidence and conclusion is that pesticides must be used to avoid a loss, which is said in C.

A is not true, B is incorrect as you can damage the environment but still increase yield, D is irrelevant to the conclusion and E is not necessarily a flaw of the argument - we don't know if it is true or not.

Question 19: E

After a 8 day holiday she is 8x3=24 days behind, starting on the 16th. For the next 14 days she recovers her fitness, being 10 days behind before the 30th, but this is when she missed 4 further sessions, meaning she is 10 + 3 x 4 = 22 days behind from the 3rd. 22 days later on the 24th she has recovered.

Question 20: B

Roughly 31250 GPs (half way between 30000 and 32500) and 12500 women. This is slightly over 1/3, so B is the only reasonable answer.

Question 21: C

Almost 50% of 12500 women were practicing full time, so 6000 is the only reasonable answer.

Question 22: D

1994 - 27500 GPs, with roughly 12% part time. So about 3500 GPs part time and 24000 full time, and if we say full time GPs work 1 hour for ease of calculation, there are $24000 + 3500 \times 0.5 = 25750$ hours.
2004 - 31250 GPs, with 25% part time, so about 7800 part time and 23500 full time. $23500 + 7800 \times 0.5 = 27400$.
With these estimates we have a percentage increase of less than 10% but this is still the best answer relative to the alternatives.

Question 23: B

Average of the guesses is $135/6 = 22.5$.
Suzie's guess is nearer than Wally's so the answer is <22 (not 22 exactly as Wally and Suzie would be equally close).
If it were 20 then Mary's guess would be closer than the average, so the answer is 21.

Question 24: C

The main idea of the passage is that H5N1 'cannot be transmitted easily between people.' Thus, in its current state, a worldwide epidemic is unlikely, but if it does mutate then this could possibly change.
A is wrong - the strain is currently not easily transmitted.
B is wrong - a mutation doesn't necessarily mean there would be a worldwide epidemic; mutations may have no/little effect, and may even have the opposite effect.
D is not correct as it is not the main idea of the passage.

Question 25: B

Let's say that 24 hours have passed.
Area covered by the minute hand = 8.4^2 x π x 12 = ~850π
Area covered by the hour hand - 6.3^2 x π = 40π
850:40 is rough ratio and only A and B are reasonable answers.
40 x 16 is much lower than 850 so 64:3 is the correct answer.

Question 26: D

The   conclusion   is   that   'nuclear   plants...are   not   needed.'
1 is correct because the argument suggests we do not need nuclear plants, but the demand for electricity may have increased, meaning they would be needed.
2 is correct because the 'huge rise in the amount these technologies add to the electricity supply' may also not continue, meaning there would be an electricity deficit.
3 is not correct because the argument is about whether nuclear plants are needed or not, so ways of storing waste are irrelevant.

Question 27: 5 hours

They walk 20km in total - 10km for one side of the journey.
Split the 10km as you wish - for example let's say there is 1km walked on flat land and 9km uphill, so in total they walk 2km on flat land, 9km down-hill and 9km up-hill.
Flat land - time = 2/4 = 30 minutes
Down-hill - time = 9/6 = 1 hour 30 minutes
Up-hill - time = 9/3 = 3 hours
Total - 5 hours.

Question 28: B

The first part of the graph is to be expected - as the population increases in year n the population increases in year n+1. However, the second part of the graph needs explaining - why there is a lower population in year n+1 if the population in year n is much higher. This is explained by B - population being too high in year n means that there in starvation, lowering the population in n+1.

A is not correct - the population would be constant if birth and death matched.

C is irrelevant, D is also not relevant as we can pick any year of the survey and this graph still holds true and E is not true - it can be falsified by the fact that a very low population in year n means a very low population in year n+1.

Question 29: D

1 is true, as we know that less glycidamide is produced in humans than in animals when acrylamide is broken down.

2 is not necessarily true - cooking at temperatures higher than 120C produces more acrylamide which could be harmful.

3 is correct - cooking them at lower temperatures means they absorb more fat and cooking them at higher temperatures means they produce more acrylamide, with an intermediate of both at mid-temperatures, so there will always be some health risks

Question 30: A

The total volume of the cube is $8 \times 8 \times 8 = 512 cm^3$. There are 8 of the 3cm cubes, which has a volume of $3 \times 3 \times 3$ each, so these take up $8 \times 27 = 216 cm^3$. The 1cm cubes on the edge overlap with the adjacent face, and there are 24 of these, taking up $24 cm^3$. There are also 20 extra for each face, taking up $6 \times 20 = 120 cm^3$ overall.

$512 - 216 - 24 - 120 = 152 cm^3$ taken up by 2cm cubes.

Each 2cm cube takes up $8 cm^3$ and $152/8 = 19$ cubes.

Question 31: B

B is the best answer - if the other companies who 'recently looked down on Google' now want to 'forge alliances', this suggests that they no longer look down on Google.

A is not necessarily true - it says Microsoft don't want this to occur, but it doesn't mean it is occurring.

C is not necessarily true - it's too bold a statement and is definitely not the only way (e.g. Microsoft could produce their own Google equivalent).

D is not necessarily true and is not a theme of the last paragraph as said in the question.

Question 32: B

You can answer this question quickly if you understand what they're asking. The revenue was boosted 80% to more than £1.2 billion, but we don't know how much more. So the revenue at the end of 2005 could have actually been any value, and we cannot put an upper limit on what this could be, so A C and D are wrong. B is therefore correct.

Question 33: C

The cartoon depicts the other companies 'ganging-up' on Google, suggesting C is correct.

A is not necessarily true - we don't know from the picture or the text that Google will 'triumph' (we don't even know what that means in this context), B is not a suitable answer, D is not true and E is not correct because the picture depicts all 3 competitors.

Question 34: C

1 is definitely true as it basically paraphrases the sentence after the conclusion given. 2 is also definitely true as it paraphrases the final sentence of this paragraph. 3 is not related to the conclusion given.

Question 35: A

Competition is a general theme of the passage, and the last sentence suggests that this 'offers opportunities for consumers.'

➢ B is too strong a statement - big companies **having** to merge -cannot be inferred.

➢ C is also too bold - the use of the word 'cannot' should put you off this answer.

➢ D cannot be inferred - we do not know what the future holds and the author does not claim to know.

➢ E is not true as the passage talks about all 4 companies competing.

END OF SECTION

Section 2

Question 1: E

Glucose is stored as glycogen in skeletal muscles and the liver. Glycogen can be broken down into glucose (glycogenolysis) to increase blood glucose levels.

Insulin decreases blood glucose by stimulating glycogen synthesis. Thus, low blood insulin will result in decreased amounts of glycogen production and increased amount of glycogenolysis.

Therefore, low blood insulin results in a decrease in glycogen mass.

NB: It's easy to over think this question (especially if you're a biochemistry graduate). Keep it simple and approach it logically.

Question 2: C

Simple molecular structures with covalent bonding normally do not conduct electricity and the melting and boiling points given are reasonable. However, they also are usually insoluble in water.

Question 3: F

2 half lives will elapse in 8 years. Thus, there will now be 8×10^{20} atoms of X. Therefore, 24×10^{20} atoms of Y will have been produced. Initial 4×10^{20} + $24 \times 10^{20} = 28 \times 10^{20}$.

Question 4: B

When you need to keep water in your body, the blood will become concentrated. In addition, ADH will be released from the posterior pituitary gland to cause more water to be reabsorbed in the distal convoluted tubule of the kidney. This in turn will cause the urine to become more concentrated.

Question 5: C

Non-metal elements get progressively more reactive as you go along a period because their electronegativity increases. Thus, the halogens are the most reactive non-metals within a period (as noble gasses are inert). Furthermore, the halogens get less reactive as you go down the group. Thus, Fluorine is the most reactive non-metal- which is shown by C.

Question 6: A

The sine and cosine rules are no longer on the BMAT Specification.

Nevertheless, this is a easy question if you draw a triangle with the values given, and then sub in the values to the cosine rule:

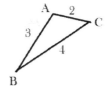

$a^2 = b^2 + c^2 - 2bc\, CosA$

$4^2 = 2^2 + 3^2 - 2\, x\, 2\, x\, 3\, CosA$

$16 = 4 + 9 - 12CosA$

$3 = -12\, CosA$

$CosA = -\frac{1}{4}$

Question 7: A

1. Microwaves are transverse waves, not longitudinal.
2. Microwaves do travel at the speed of light in air.
3. Ultrasound is used in pre-natal scanning
4. Infrared light is used for thermal imaging.
5. All types of electromagnetic radiation, including microwaves can travel through a vacuum.

Question 8: C

Since, 165 is the upper quartile, 25% of people will have a heart rate greater than 165. Thus, the probability of an individual having a heart rate over 165 is = ¼

There are 4 possible permutations for 3 members having a HR > 165 and 1 < 165 (the member with a HR under 165 could be in any position). Thus, the probability of this:

$$= \frac{1}{4} x \frac{1}{4} x \frac{1}{4} x \frac{3}{4} \ x \ 4 \ = \frac{12}{256}$$

The Probability of 4 members having a HR > 165:

$$= \frac{1}{4} x \frac{1}{4} x \frac{1}{4} x \frac{1}{4} \ x \ 4 \ = \frac{1}{256}$$

Total probability = $\frac{12}{256} + \frac{1}{256} = \frac{13}{256}$

Question 9: B

1. Catalysts don't affect the position of equilibrium, so will not change yield.
2. Adding more reactant will shift the equilibrium towards the products.
3. Increasing the pressure will shift the equilibrium towards the products because the reactants have two moles of gas and the products have one mole of gas.
4. Increasing the temperature will favour the reverse endothermic reaction which will decrease the salt yield.

Question 10: D

Firstly, note that only 75% of the plants survived and this is unlikely to be due to chance given the sample size. Now, let **A** be the dominant allele and let **a** be the recessive allele.

	A	**a**
A	$AA(\frac{1}{3})$	$Aa(\frac{1}{3})$
a	$Aa(\frac{1}{3})$	aa (dead)

As can be seen, 2 out the 3 surviving plants are heterozygotes = 67%.

Question 11: C

There is actually no need to do any maths here! Pressures across fluids are transmitted so the pressure at X = pressure transmitted to Y.

Question 12: E

$$r = 1 - \frac{6\sum d^2}{n(n^2-1)}$$

$$r - 1 = -\frac{6\sum d^2}{n^3 - n}$$

$$1 - r = \frac{6}{n^3 - n}\sum d^2$$

$$\sum d^2 = \frac{(1-r)(n^3 - n)}{6}$$

Question 13: B

The 'loss in mass' = Mass of Product Gasses

The 'loss in mass' = Mass of $KHCO_3$ – Mass of K_2CO_3

M_r of the $KHCO_3$ = $39 + 1 + 12 + 3 \times 16 = 100$

Number of Moles of $KHCO_3 = \frac{50}{100} = 0.5\ moles$

The molar ratio between $KHCO_3$ and K_2CO_3 is 2:1. Thus, two moles of $KHCO_3$ react with one mole of K_2CO_3.

M_r of the $K_2CO_3 = 2 \times 39 + 12 + 3 \times 16 = 138$

Mass of $K_2CO_3 = 0.25 \times 138 = 34.5g$

The 'loss in mass' = $50 - 34.5 = 15.5g$

Question 14: x = 3, y = 1

$4x^2 + y^2 + 10y = 47\ and\ 2x - y = 5$

Thus, $y = 2x - 5$. Substitute into the first equation to give:

$4x^2 + (2x - 5)^2 + 10(2x - 5) = 47$

$4x^2 + (4x^2 - 20x + 25) + (20x - 50) = 47$

$8x^2 - 25 = 47$

$8x^2 = 72$

$x^2 = 9$

Since we want the positive solutions only; $x = 3$

Substitute back in to give: $y = 2x - 5 = 6 - 5 = 1$

Question 15: E

➢ Urea is produced when proteins are broken down in the liver, so the highest concentration will be at 3.
➢ Starch/long carbohydrates are broken down into sugar monomers in the stomach and intestines so glucose concentration will be highest at 2.
➢ Oxygen will be lowest in 3 because blood has travelled through more organs (and therefore oxygen has been used up the most).

Question 16: $2m/s^2$

Resultant force = Force from pulleys – Weight

Resultant force $= 120 \; x \; 2 - 20 \; x \; 10 = 40 \; N$

Now using, $F = ma$; $40 = 20a$

Thus, $a = 2 \; ms^{-2}$

Question 17: E

1. The nucleus has a relative mass of 40.
2. It is not a noble gas as it has a configuration of 2,8,8,2 and thus has 2 electrons in the outer shell.
3. It has 2 electrons in the outer shell. Therefore, it would lose 2 electrons to obtain the noble gas configuration, hence it would form a positive ion.
4. The element has 2 electrons in the outer shell so it is in group 2.
5. The element is in group 2 which are the alkali metals.

Question 18: C

➢ The student takes 14 x 4 = 56 breaths in 4 minutes.
➢ Each breath is 0.5 dm^3 so 56 breaths = 56 x 0.5 = 28 dm^3
➢ The percentage of oxygen absorbed = 21 – 16 = 5%
➢ Thus, amount of oxygen absorbed = 5% of 28 dm^3 = 1.4 dm^3

Question 19: C

This is no longer on the BMAT syllabus.
The pupil dilates when the light levels decrease to allow more light in. This is accomplished by contraction of the radial muscles and relaxation of the circular muscles.

Question 20: E

You are no longer expected to be able to calculate resistances & voltages in parallel circuits for the BMAT. However, it's important that you understand the principles involved with parallel circuits as they do frequently come up.

➢   The voltage across both branches is equal.
➢   The upper branch (series) has a greater resistance than the lower branch (parallel).
➢   Since, $I = \frac{V}{R}$, the current in the upper branch is smaller than the lower branch.

Now using V = IR, we can see that there is a greater voltage running through R2 than R1.

Since the voltage splits evenly across the second branch point in the lower branch, R3 has half the voltage of R2.

Therefore, the potential difference in ascending order is: R3 → R1 → R2.

Question 21: 9

$$= \left(\frac{32^{\frac{1}{5}} + 9^0}{81^{\frac{3}{4}}} \right)^{-1}$$

$$= \left(\frac{2+1}{3^3} \right)^{-1}$$

$$= \left(\frac{3}{27} \right)^{-1}$$

$$= \left(\frac{1}{9} \right)^{-1} = 9$$

Question 22: D
A. The activation energy is represented by V + W.
B. Y shows the route taken in the presence of a catalyst (not X).
C. The reaction is endothermic as the energy of the products is greater than the energy of the reactants.
D. Correct.

Question 23: C

The frequency of light doesn't change during refraction.

Blue light has a higher wavelength than red light (it's just one of those facts you need to know!). Since $c = f\lambda$, the speed of blue light must be less than the speed of red light in glass.

Question 24: E

1. Correct – aerobic respiration releases far more energy than anaerobic respiration.
2. Incorrect- Oxygen debt can only occur in the presence of anaerobic respiration.
3. Incorrect – Aerobic respiration also produces water as a waste product.
4. Correct- active transport requires ATP which would be less available if there were reduced aerobic respiration.
5. Incorrect - the muscles will still use any oxygen available for aerobic respiration.
6. Correct – lactate is the only waste product of anaerobic respiration.

Question 25: B

This is no longer on the syllabus.

Don't get bogged down in the equations. 4 protons fuse to create a helium nucleus which consists of 2 protons and 2 neutrons. Therefore, 2 of the original 4 protons have to be converted into neutrons – hence B.

Question 26: A

The best way to do these is to express the relationships algebraically: $A \ \alpha \ \frac{1}{b^2}$

Therefore $A = \frac{k}{b^2}$

Substitute the values in to give: $9 = \frac{k}{4^2}$

Therefore, $k = 9 \ x \ 16 = 144$

When A = 4; $4 = \frac{144}{b^2}$

$b^2 = 36$

$b = 6$

Question 27: 5 seconds

Charge per unit surface area = $0.25C/m^2$ and the surface area = $0.04m^2$

Therefore, the overall charge = $0.04 \ x \ 0.25 = 0.01 \ C$

Recall that $Charge = current \ x \ time$

$Time = \frac{10^{-2}}{2 \ x \ 10^{-3}}$

$\frac{1}{2 \ x \ 10^{-1}} = \frac{1}{0.2}$

$= 5 \ seconds$

END OF SECTION

Section 3

Our zeal to make things work better will not be our anthem: it will be our epitaph. (Appleyard)

➢ Appleyard suggests that our drive to improve things will not be our success, but our downfall.

➢ Many researchers believe that it is not long before artificial intelligence achieves the storage capacity and processing speed of the human brain. A huge number of science fiction films portray this leading to robotic being sentient and conscious, such as Terminator and I.Robot, but even unconscious machines may have the ability to transcend humanity. It is likely that these machines would have the ability to replicate themselves more efficiently than humans.

➢ If machines had the ability to make their own decisions then one could argue that the fate of the human race would be at the mercy of these robots. Even if this was not the case, however, we may become so dependent on technology that we essentially become 'engineered' and completely lose our freedom.

➢ Talking in the present, modern technology and our insatiable desire to 'make things better' is undoubtedly causing problems such as global warming and loss of resources which will potentially have a devastating long term effect. Furthermore, rapid technological advancement has clearly led to a more stressful and fast paced lifestyle, and many epidemiologists believe that this is the cause of the exponential rise in mental health issues in the last 50 years (there is certainly, at least, a correlation).

➢ However, the only way to deal with problems such as global warming and mental health is further innovative technology, to try and find renewable, environmentally-friendly sources of energy and treatments to aid those with psychological problems.

➢ Technology is often crucial to our survival; if the Earth was to be subject to a global natural disaster, only technology would allow us to propel into space and find a new method of surviving. From a medical perspective, only new technology would be able to save us from a devastating new virus that is readily transmitted and fatal when contracted. Even on a very current basis, antibiotics need constant innovation or natural resistance would render them useless.

Higher education and great numbers - that is a contradiction in terms. (Nietzsche)

➢ Nietzsche suggests that higher education should be reserved for only a small proportion of a population, who have earned the right and privilege for further study through merit. It follows on from the idea that the greatest things in life cannot be common property.

➢ Indeed, it could be argued that overcrowded institutions with overworked teachers/professors leads to a lower quality of education which is detrimental to all. Higher education should be students who are the 'cream of the crop,' taught by those were once the 'cream of the crop,' whereas with a high number of students there is a mediocrity to the teaching and what is achieved. Also, as there are more students to teach who are not exclusively a talented an motivated academic group, bad teaching cannot be survived.

➢ Higher education is commonly thought of as university, and the government has always been keen to ensure that this is not an elitist system, although the recent rise in tuition fees may suggest otherwise. However, although most 18 year old studying for their A Levels are encouraged to go to university, Nietzsche may believe that only those who have the ability to be the very best and who are keen to specialise in a precise academic area should proceed to further education.

➢ Indeed, students often see higher education as the only way to establish a career, often meaning that the essence of 'education' itself is lost. Universities, more and more, are entering a time of commodification and marketization and we should only accept high numbers in higher education if it benefits society as a whole. How universities are run now may detract from essential 'academic' work that needs to be done.

➢ However, education as a notion is subjective and the view of Nietzsche is certainly not a general one. For many, the employability factor of higher education is huge, and for them this is a legitimate reason to pursue further study.

➢ It can be argued that education should be a right at any level. Some may use higher education to train for a future career. Some may use it to improve society for the better and may use it to ensure that we all have a future.

➢ Indeed, over time we have had a fundamental change of university from an elite system to a mass system, and it has, on the whole, appeared a success. It allows education to go beyond your social class, race and other factors and allows equal opportunity. Students are more demanding in this age regularly criticise the teaching and learning support they get, and the education received, even though by a larger number of people, has certainly improved over the years.

The main benefit of patient consent is that it relieves doctors of blame for bad decisions.

- ➤ The statement suggests that, if a patient has given their permission for a treatment to go ahead, then the doctor cannot be attributable if the treatment doesn't go to plan.
- ➤ Although this may be true to an extent, the reason that patient consent is a main idea of Good Medical Practice issued by the GMC is that it benefits the patient and respects their autonomy.
- ➤ Valid, informed consent requires competence (right mind), non-coercion (right person) and information (right understanding). No consent is battery (a crime).
- ➤ There are many benefits of patient consent, the most obvious being the transmission of information from someone who has knowledge (the physician) to someone who does not (the patient), so that the patient is fully aware of what the treatment involves, the risks and benefits, whether there are alternative treatments and what may happen if treatment does not go ahead. It also respect patient autonomy and allows competent patients to control what happens to their body. It also protects the patient's right of self-determination and engages the patient in their own healthcare.
- ➤ A competent patient can decide if they want to endure chemotherapy as their cancer treatment, or whether they would like to take part in a clinical trial to try and alleviate their Parkinson's disease. However, recent Mental Health Acts protect patients that lack the capacity to make decisions for themselves, and discusses how decisions should be made in their best interests.
- ➤ Ultimately, in most cases, if patients have a clear appreciation and understanding of the facts, implications, and consequences of a treatment/action, they are free to choose as they wish.

END OF PAPER

2007

Section 1

Question 1: B

After 1 year the tree is 1m tall.
The max is 30m, so the difference between the height and the max is 29m.
10% of this is 2.9m, so after 2 years, the tree is $1 + 2.9 = 3.9$m tall.
The difference now is 26.1m, 10% of this is 2.6m (answer is 1dp), so after 3 years, the tree is $3.9 + 2.6 = 6.5$m tall.

Question 2: C

The argument discusses how WMDs are not the only means through which people are killed in warfare. C thus logically follows the idea that they are not unique in their ability to cause destruction. This is further emphasised in the last line.
'200,000 people were killed...by the atomic bombs' which suggests the WMDs are 'morally unacceptable,' 'a serious threat' and 'necessarily devastating'.

Question 3: C

Find out the increase for each representative - A 60000, B 40000, C 50000, D 100000, E 50000. You should then be able to work out that answer C is correct - for example, Darwin should have 1/3 of the pie chart because his increase is 100000, out of a total increase of 300000.

Question 4: A

The argument suggests that a higher level of mastery should be required to pass a test, which would then reduce the loss of young life. However, it does not consider that young male drivers may already be highly skilled and still be involved in accidents, as said in 1.

2 and 3 do not weaken the argument - the argument that we should increase the threshold for driving skills before allowing one to pass to prevent road deaths, still has high validity with these considerations. 2 is irrelevant to the skill of the driver and 3 actually supports the argument.

Question 5: B

From the answers given, we can see that the percentage occupancy is 92853/109505 for acute, 24291/26619 for geriatric, 27832/31667 for mental illness, 4134/4899 for learning disabilities and 5737/9095 for maternity. Hopefully you can immediately see that maternity is too low. If we call the rest 93/110, 24.3/26.6, 27.8/31.7 and 4.1/4.9, you can hopefully see that 24.3/26.6 is the largest. 93/110 is roughly 23/27.5 (divide by 4) which is clearly smaller than 24.3/26.6. 24.3/26.6 is larger than 27.8/31.7 - 24.3 to 27.8 is a 15% increase but the denominator increase is much larger. 4.1/4.9 is around 24/30 which is also clearly larger than 24.3/26.6.

Question 6: B

1 is correct because the headline suggests there is a growing digital divide, whereas the survey only found values for social networking. 2 is correct because to show a gap is growing, you also need an earlier survey. 3 is not related to the question, because it is nothing to do with the headline.

Question 7: E

Let's say the first bulb is red - this has a 3/6 chance. With the sequence we want: the next bulb has a 3/5 chance of being yellow, the next has a 2/4 chance of being red, the next has a 2/3 chance of being yellow, the next has a ½ chance of being red and the final one has a 1/1 chance of being yellow.

So 3/6 x 3/5 x 2/4 x 2/3 x ½ x 1 = 1/20.
However, we must multiply this value by 2 because there are 2 permutations - the first bulb could be yellow, and then alternate by there. 1/10.

Question 8: C

The passage begins with 'many people think that if they cannot explain something, it must therefore be truly paranormal,' but the author goes on to criticise this by giving examples of where this thinking has been wrong, which suggests C is the correct answer.
A and B are too bold to be inferred and D doesn't have a definite basis.

Question 9: E

2kg cat - ber = 30 x 2 + 70 = 130. mer = 130 x 1.6 = 208 kcal/day
Requires 7g per 100kcal, so 14g per 200kcal, and 0.56g per 8kcal, so the total required is 14 + 0.56 = 14.56 - E is correct.

Question 10: C

ber for this cat is 70, and the mer is 70 x 1.3 = 91kcal/day. It requires 7g/100kcal of protein and thus requires 6.3g for 91kcal. CCFR has 0.06g/ml and 1kcal/ml, so dividing the former by the latter gives us 0.06g/kcal (ml cancels) which is 6g/100kcal. This means it gets 5.4g for 91kcal, which is 0.9g short.

~ 103 ~

Question 11: C

A cat with renal failure requires 4g/100kcal.
FCH has 1.4g/1.3kcal which is far too high.
CCFR has 0.06g/1kcal which is 6g/100kcal - too high.
ES has 0.04g/1kcal which is 4g/100kcal - correct.
OHN has 0.05g/1.1kcal which is 5g/110kcal - too high.
EMF has 0.08g/2.1kcal which is 8g/210kcal - too low.

Question 12: C

Ratio of protein to energy required is 6:100. Call the volume of ES added E.

100ml x 0.09 + 0.04E = 0.06(100+E)
9 + 0.04E = 6 + 0.06E
3 = 0.02E
300 = 2E. Therefore, E = 150ml

Question 13: C

The graph shows the percentage who had drunk on x days or more, and our percentage for all ages is about 18%. From the table: if this is 3 days or more, then we would have a percentage of 10 + 6 + 4 +3 + 11 = 34% - too high. If this is 6 days or more, then we have a percentage of 3 + 11 = 14% - too low. If this is 5 days or more, then we have a percentage of 4 + 3 + 11 = 17% - correct.

Question 14: A

The argument suggests that dogs' excellent hearing ability means they can hear sounds that occur before an earthquake, which increases their anxiety. A supports this argument because it suggests that dogs that haven't got this hearing ability did not hear the sound and thus did not show an increase in anxiety.
B is irrelevant to why dogs in particular increase in anxiety, C does not necessarily give support to the argument stated above and D weakens the argument by suggesting there are no pre-earthquake sounds.

Question 15: C

If A got 1/3, P and E got 2/3 combined, so $2x/3 = 174$ if x is the total number of votes. $x = 261$, so $x/3 = 87$. Paul wins by $116 - 87 = 29$ votes.

Question 16: A

The conclusion of the argument is the last line "someone who is awarded a PhD in Sweden will live longer." The only data we are given is that those aged 64 with a PhD were less likely to die within the next year than those with a BA, BSc or MA, so we cannot definitely infer that what is true for this general group is true for each individual, which is the assumption made.

B is not correct as there is nothing said about a healthy lifestyle in the argument.
C is not correct because the conclusion states those in SWEDEN will live longer, so there is no assumption about other.
D is a statement that shows an error of reasoning and the assumption is only the other way around to what is stated here.

Question 17: B

Only 2 is correct - the argument suggests that smokers are more addicted to nicotine now because they inhale, in total, a larger amount of nicotine. However, this statement suggests that the nicotine inhaled isn't necessary increased (because less cigarettes are smoked in total, despite the increase per cigarette), which weakens the argument.
1 is irrelevant to the amount of nicotine involved.
3 doesn't weaken the argument about smokers being more addicted due to increased nicotine.

Question 18: B

Paving slabs have an area of 70 x 70 = 4900 cm^2 or 0.49m^2. Bob can buy 50 slabs with £140. 50 x 0.49 = 24.5m^2 can be covered with this.

The area covered is twice as long as it is wide. Area = x * 2x slabs, 50 = 2x^2 so x = 10 - the length is 10m and the width is 5m.

IF we have 10 slabs along length and 5 slabs along the width, this covers 5 x 70cm + 10 x 70cm = 3.5m^2 x 7m^2 covered by the slabs.

Flowerbed width = 5m^2 - 3.5m^2 = 1.5m^2

Question 19: B

Car 1 gets 4 seconds ahead of car 2 per lap - 4 seconds after lap 1, 8 after lap 2, 12 after lap 3 etc. When car 1 laps car 2, it fulfils the criteria that 66s x number of laps = 70 x (number of laps - 1). This expands to give 70 = 4 x number of laps, so it takes 17.5 laps. 17.5 laps x 66 seconds gives 1155 seconds which is 19 minutes and 15 seconds.

Question 20: D

Out of 1000 men we know 21 are screen with a true positive and 85 are screened with a false positive. This is 106/1000 men screened positive with DRE, which is 10.6%.

Question 21: C

Draw a tree diagram here. Either men have an abnormal PSA level (0.1 chance) and have prostate cancer (0.26 chance), giving a 0.1 x 0.26 = 0.026 = 2.6% chance this way. Or, men could have a normal PSA level (0.9 chance) and be a false negative (0.008 chance), giving a 0.9 x 0.008 = 0.0072 = 0.72% chance this way. 2.6 + 0.72 = 3.3%.

Question 22: A

1 is correct. PSA gives 0.1 x 0.74 false positives, which is 0.074 = 7.4%. DRE gives 85/1000 false positives which is 8.5% - this is higher. 2 is also correct. PSA gives 0.9 x 0.008 false negatives, which is 0.72%. DRE gives 16/1000 false positives, which is 1.6% - this is again higher.

Question 23: B

Chance of a false positive on PSA is 0.074, chance on DRE is 0.085. 0.074 x 0.085 = 0.00629 (do 74 x 85 and then work it out from there), which is 0.6% - on average 6/1000 would have false positives on both.

Question 24: D

The conclusion, 'what really drives globalisation is the availability of cheap air travel and cheap shipping,' suggests that the internet is neither necessary nor sufficient for globalisation. If it were sufficient, the argument would suggest that the internet alone, without this shipping etc., could lead to globalisation. If it were necessary, the argument would suggest that the shipping/travel isn't possible without the internet.

Question 25: B

Ethanol is currently (2007) produced on 54,000 square km of farmland, which needs to increase to 334,000 by 2017 to meet the target. This would give 334000 + 54000 = 388000 square kilometres in 2017. This is just over 7x more than in 2007 (54 x 7 = 378) so if we can produce 35 billion gallons in 2017, we produce just over 7 times less now. 35/7 = 5, and because our denominator is slightly more than 7, we get 4.9 billion gallons.

Question 26: C

There are only 4 combinations that are possible here, and 2 of them result in Q and R sitting next to each other.

1. Window (O) (N) (M) aisle (P) ( ) ( ) which leaves Q and R to sit next to each other.
2. Window ( ) ( ) (P) aisle (M) (N) (O) which also leaves Q and R to sit next to each other.
3. Window ( ) (M) (N) aisle (P) ( ) (O) which doesn't let Q and R sit next to each other.
4. Window (O) ( ) (P) aisle (N) (M) ( ) which doesn't let Q and R sit next to each other.

Question 27: C

6/50 had rings on them when rounded up, and 50 have rings overall. So 6/50 = 50/x, x = 50 x 50/6 = ~417.

Question 28: A

The data suggests a correlation between the being light on during sleep and myopia in children, and the conclusion is that there is causality between these 2 factors. A gives another way that these 2 factors may be linked - the fact that myopic parents leave the children's light on more often, so the causal factor actually being the transfer of myopic-related genes.

B, C and D are not flaws because they do not give an alternative explanation for the correlation.

Question 29: C

The first sentence defines conflict diamonds: 'sold in order to finance the military rebellion of groups opposing recognised governments,' and the conclusion suggests that the cost of these are too high for 'war-torn countries.' However, C weakens this, suggesting that the sale of these diamonds actually helps the recognised governments of war-torn countries.

Not knowing where a diamond originates does not weaken the argument that the diamond is an unnecessary luxury and has too high a cost, so we can rule out A. B has nothing to do with diamonds, and the significance of diamonds mentioned in D has nothing to do with diamonds in the context of war/governments.

Question 30: E

Visualisation - cut the shapes out and try it yourself if you want. The triangles will fold to form squares in Q and S, but not P and R.

Question 31: B

MHR= $217 - 0.85 \times 60 = 217 - 51 = 166$.
Add 4 beats for 55+ elite athletes - $166 + 4 = 170$.
Subtract 14 beats for swimming training - $170 - 14 = 156$

Question 32: D

A and B are not correct - we don't know anything about absolute wages, only proportions.
C is not correct - for example the wage proportion for women in education after 21/22 (relative to those leaving education at 15) follows a general downward trend.
D is correct - this is suggested by the downward trend seen for women at 21/22.
E cannot be inferred - we only have proportions relative to those who left education at 15.

Question 33: C

This is yet another correlation does not mean causation question. A general positive correlation is seen between wage increase and years of education past 15, and the authors assume a causality.

With averages there is no assumption that some outliers are not biasing the data, so A is wrong. B is irrelevant as the graph is about relative wages, not absolute wages. D is not an assumption made - it is actually a potential counter argument. E is clearly wrong.

Question 34: B

We have a link between being a trade union member and having lower financial returns for a degree, and we want a cause. B suggests a reason why trade union membership may mean less money.

A is irrelevant as the number of people that get trade union membership doesn't provide a reason for the link. C is wrong because we are talking about those that do have a degree. D is wrong because age is irrelevant here. E is wrong for the same reason as A.

Question 35: D

The fact that older people left education earlier but earned more actually counters the general trend in our graph, so without this, the correlation we see would be much stronger. Thus the effect is that it lowers the gradient of the graph, weakening the link.

END OF SECTION

Section 2

Question 1: B

Proteins are normally found in the blood but do not pass through the glomerulus after ultrafiltration (so A is wrong), giving an filtrate that is mainly water.

As we carry on through the kidney, more water is reabsorbed and glucose is completely reabsorbed, making the fluid more concentrated with urea. Since there is still some glucose and very little urea, this sample must be from the proximal convoluted tubule which is represented by B.

Question 2: B

A. If x was in groups 3 to 8, y would be in the third period.
B. Since x is in the second period, and y is in the second/third period, this means that both must have at least 2 electrons in their first shell.
C. Element y would only have 6 more electrons in its outer most shell if x was in group 1 or 2.
D. Since y has 6 more protons, it will likely also have a few neutrons in addition as well. Thus, the nucleon number of y will be greater than that of x by more than 6.

Question 3: α=220, β=40

Only 60 counts pass through the sheet of paper, which is 40 when we account for the background. Only β radiation passes through a sheet of paper, so this value is 40.

The count rate is 280 at the start = 260 once adjusted for background radiation. If 40 of these counts are caused by β then 220 must be caused by α particles.

Question 4: A

The adjusted equation is: $A = \dfrac{(1.5x + 1.5y)^2 \times 0.8z \times Q}{2P}$

$A = \dfrac{1.5^2(x+y)^2 \times 0.8z \times Q}{2P}$

Since we are only interested in the percentage change, we can ignore the unknown variables:

$A = \dfrac{(1.5)^2 \times 0.8}{2}$

$A = 2.25 \times 0.4 = 0.9$

Thus, A has decreased by 10%.

Question 5: E

During expiration, the ribs move down and inwards (hold your ribs when exhaling if you're not sure!). The diaphragm muscles relax during expiration, not contract. The pressure in the lungs increases during expiration, so that a pressure gradient is created which causes air to move out.

Question 6: A

$t = 2\pi\sqrt{\dfrac{2lR^2\left(W+\frac{w}{3}\right)}{n\pi r^4 g}}$

$\left(\dfrac{t}{2\pi}\right)^2 = \dfrac{2lR^2\left(W+\frac{w}{3}\right)}{n\pi r^4 g}$

$\dfrac{n\pi r^4 g}{2lR^2} \times \left(\dfrac{t}{2\pi}\right)^2 = \left(W+\dfrac{w}{3}\right)$

$W = \dfrac{n\pi r^4 g}{2lR^2} \times \dfrac{t^2}{4\pi^2} - \dfrac{w}{3}$

$W = \dfrac{nr^4 g t^2}{8l\pi R^2} - \dfrac{w}{3}$

Question 7: 300

Using $P = IV$, the output voltage $= \frac{0.5 \times 10^3}{10} = 50\ V$

Then, input these values into: $\frac{V_p}{V_s} = \frac{n_p}{n_s}$

$\frac{250}{50} = \frac{1500}{x}$

$x = \frac{1500}{5} = 300$

Question 8: B

In Fe_3O_4, the O has a redox state of -2, so O_4 has a redox state of -8. The compound is electrically neutral thus Fe_3 must consist of 2 atoms in the +3 state and 1 in the +2 state. Thus $\frac{1}{3}$ is in the +2 state.

Note that Fe_3O_4 couldn't consist of 4 atoms in the +2 states because the question specifically states that the oxide contains both Fe^{2+} and Fe^{3+}.

Question 9: B

Blood is pumped from the right ventricle to the lungs and from the left ventricle to the body. Both of these processes happen at the same time. Thus, the atrio-ventricular valves are closed on both sides to prevent backflow into the ventricles and the semilunar valves are open to allow blood flow into the pulmonary artery + aorta.

Question 10: D

The greatest number of moles of reactants produces the most precipitate. Since one mole lead iodide precipitate reacts with two moles of potassium iodide, we need to double the moles of KI in the calculations.

A. $\dfrac{5}{1000} \times 2 + 2 \times \dfrac{10}{1000} \times 2 = 0.03 \; moles$

B. $\dfrac{2.5}{1000} \times 5 + 2 \times \dfrac{2.5}{1000} \times 2.5 = 0.0375 \; moles$

C. $\dfrac{7.5}{1000} \times 3 + 2 \times \dfrac{5}{1000} \times 5 = 0.0725 \; moles$

D. $\dfrac{5}{1000} \times 4 + 2 \times \dfrac{7.5}{1000} \times 5 = 0.095 \; moles$

A good student would spend little time working out the values; they would see that the value of D would be the highest just by inspection.

Question 11: E

A. A substance can lose heat energy without its temperature falling if it is changing state.
B. Thermal radiation can pass through a vacuum.
C. Steam has more heat energy at the same temperature as boiling water because the intermolecular bonds in the boiling water are still unbroken.
D. Cooling or heating a container of water will set up a convection current, regardless of the location.

Question 12: E

850 steps is the mean and 1000 steps is the upper quartile value, so ¼ of the sample have values within this range.

3 members having a value within this range has a probability:

$$= \frac{1}{4} \times \frac{1}{4} \times \frac{1}{4} = \frac{1}{64}$$

Question 13: C

This is no longer on the BMAT syllabus.
The fulcrum acts as a pivot. If you stand on your toes, then the calf muscles contract, and the upwards force from the calf is the effort. The downward force is the load, and this is between the pivot and effort.

Question 14: A

Elements further down in group 1 are more reactive, and elements further up in group 7 are more reactive. Thus, the element on top of group 7 (Fluorine) and on the bottom of group 1 (Caesium) will react extremely violently. This will therefore be the most exothermic reaction.

Question 15: B

This is no longer on the BMAT syllabus.

➤ The refracted rays of light will follow similar trajectories – this excludes out C & D.
➤ Since light is incident in the top half of the bubble, it will leave from the top of the bubble as well. This excludes E & F.
➤ The wavelength of red light is higher than that of violet. Thus, red light undergoes less refraction than violet light.
➤ Hence, the answer is B.

Question 16: C

The quickest way to do this is to substitute in the values to see if they satisfy the inequality:

➤ $(-1, -6)$: $-6 \geq 1 + 3$ is incorrect
➤ $(2, -1)$: $-1 \geq 4 + 3$ is incorrect
➤ $(1, 6)$: $6 \geq 1 + 3$ and $1 \geq \frac{1}{6}$. This is correct for both.
➤ $(2, 2)$: $2 \geq 4 + 3$ is incorrect

Question 17: D

We first deduce that this is a sex linked condition based on who gets the syndrome. Call the alleles X^N for the faulty gene and X^n for the normal gene.

The male in the first generation has a genotype of $X^N Y$ so he passes on his X^N gene to both his daughters, 8 and 9. The mother must provide the X^n to both otherwise they would have the condition.

This leaves answers D and E. We cannot deduce anything about 5, but we know 4 is heterozygous. 3 must have a genotype of $X^h Y$, otherwise he would have the condition. 4 must have a genotype of $X^H X^h$ - if she were homozygous dominant then she would have the condition and if she were homozygous recessive then she would not be able to have offspring with the condition.

Question 18: D

Moles of water $= \frac{mass}{Mr} = \frac{6}{18} = \frac{1}{3} \ moles.$

1 mole of gas occupies 24,000 cm^3.

Thus, $\frac{1}{3}$ moles occupy $24000 \ x \frac{1}{3} = 8000 \ cm^3$

Question 19: 700N

This is a difficult question as it requires a couple of conceptual leaps:

The bar is in equilibrium so: Moments clockwise = moments anti-clockwise

The bar exerts its weight in the midpoint between the pivot and the bar's end. Let y be the weight of the bar:

$1000 \ x \ 1.5 + \frac{1.5}{2} y = 4.5 \ x \ 100 + \frac{4.5}{2} y$
$1500 + 0.75 \ y = 450 + 2.25 \ y$
$1050 = 1.5 \ y$
$y = 700N$

Question 20: A

Using Pythagoras' Theorem: $a^2 = c^2 - b^2$

$$a^2 = \left(6 + \sqrt{5}\right)^2 - \left(3 + 2\sqrt{5}\right)^2$$
$$a^2 = (36 + 12\sqrt{5} + 5) - \left(9 + 12\sqrt{5} + 20\right)$$
$$a^2 = 36 + 12\sqrt{5} + 5 - 9 - 12\sqrt{5} - 20$$
$$a^2 = 12$$
$$a = \sqrt{12}$$
$$a = \sqrt{4} \times \sqrt{3}$$
$$a = 2\sqrt{3}$$

Question 21: E

Platelets are responsible for clotting, so a decreased platelet count means less clotting. White blood cells mediate immune responses so abnormal white blood cells means reduced disease resistance. There is no information about red blood cells so we can assume oxygen transport is normal.

Question 22: D

1. Correct - NH_3 is the correct formula of ammonia.
2. Incorrect - Ammonia is a weak alkali in H_2O and thus has a pH > 7.
3. Correct - Ammonia has a molecular structure.
4. Incorrect - Ammonia is a base so turns damp litmus paper blue.
5. Incorrect - Ammonia is a gas at room temperature
6. Correct - Ammonia is covalently bonded.

Question 23: E

Let the cross sectional area be A. The section of an artery can be modelled as a cylinder with a volume Ax.

The volume of blood flowing through the artery in one second is the same as the volume of the artery divided by the time it takes for a single RBC to pass through its length:

$$V = \frac{Ax}{T}, so\ A = \frac{Vx}{T}$$

However, the units for this would be ml/mm, and we want the cross sectional area in mm^2. Since $1\ ml = 1\ mm^3$, we must multiply by 10^3 to get the final answer = $A = \frac{Vx}{T}\ x\ 10^3$

Question 24: A

Volume of the hemisphere $= \frac{4}{3}\pi r^3\ x\ \frac{1}{2} = \frac{2}{3}\pi r^3$

Volume of the cylinder $= \pi r^2 l$

Total volume $= \frac{2}{3}\pi r^3 + \pi r^2 l$

$= \pi r^2 (\frac{2}{3}r + l)$

$= \frac{\pi r^2}{3}(2r + 3l)$

Question 25: A

The top of a fractionating column is where the hydrocarbon with the lowest boiling point fractions off, which will be at 68^0C. The temperature in the flask would be the average of both boiling points, which is 83^0C.

Question 26: C

This is no longer on the BMAT syllabus.
Oestrogen causes the lining of the uterus to thicken, progesterone maintains the lining of the uterus (e.g. during pregnancy), and a fall in progesterone causes the lining of the uterus to break down (causing bleeding in the menstrual cycle).

Question 27: D

Beta radiation involves a neutron transforming into a high energy electron and a proton. Thus, the atomic number increases by one, so 1 is correct. The tumour is attacked by gamma radiation, but the radiation attacks all cells, not just malignant cells.

END OF SECTION

Section 3

The technology of medicine has outrun its sociology.

➤ The author suggests that we have reached a stage whereby the technology of medicine has exceeded our current ability to apply it effectively as a society.

➤ Sigerist may be referring to the fact that portions of society regularly reject medical technologies due to religious, cultural or even personal beliefs, highlighting that the sociology is running behind the technology.

➤ It could also be argued that this statement refers to the notion the availability of clinical technological advancements are limited to a portion of society, independent of the people's views of the technology. Many treatments are only available privately, favouring the rich who can afford them, thus suggesting that the focus on technology has superseded the GMC's first rule of good practice: "make the care of you patient your primary concern."

➤ The technology of using embryonic stem cells can be used to, for example, make new brain cells to treat Parkinson's disease, help to replace damaged heart valves or help to rebuild cartilage and clearly has a huge range of potential applications as they can specialise into any cell. However, in order to obtain embryonic stem cells, the early embryo has to be destroyed which some regard as destroying a potential human life, and there is hence much controversy around this area and much of society does not accept this technology. Adult stem cells also exist, but these can only develop into a smaller subset of cells.

➤ To address this problem, researchers have tried to find ways to obtain embryonic stem cells without having to destroy the embryos. Methods to do this include deriving stem cells from mice embryos, and reprogramming adult stem cells to act more like embryonic stem cells - these are called induced pluripotent stem cells.

Our unprecedented survival has produced a revolution in longevity which is shaking the foundations of societies around the world and profoundly altering our attitudes to life and death

➢ Improvements in healthcare and medicine mean we have defied nature to levels that were not previously possible, which the statement suggests has affected our lifestyles and has changed our outlooks and approaches regarding life and death.

➢ Our longevity has caused overpopulation, despite a limited and finite number of resources, putting more pressure and demands on the Earth and causing increased famine and poor quality of life for some.

➢ In this country, the increased longevity has meant an ageing population who must be supported by a younger generation, putting a burden on public funds. Also, technology has led to many ethical issues about life and death, such as for how long we should keep someone on a life support machine.

➢ Furthermore, our longevity has meant people fear death less, at least in the sense of contracting a disease or illness that we consider minor now but may have been fatal many years ago. Indeed, the current obsession with risky activities such as extreme sports is probably borne from this fact, with people confident that they will recover even if something goes wrong.

➢ However, the fear of unknowns such as death still undoubtedly continues for most, and the way we treat the dead (burial, cremation etc.) has remained constant throughout history, despite longevity extending. Many societies are not experiencing this increase in longevity anyway, such as third world countries - can we definitely say their attitudes have changed?

➢ Basic human nature and lifestyles have not necessarily been 'shaken' by this increase. We are still governed by laws, we still survive through basic necessities such as food, warmth and we then must reproduce, and our attitudes and opinions towards many factors are the same.

Irrationally held truths may be more harmful than reasoned errors. (Huxley)

➤ This seemingly paradoxical statement is essentially about the concept of epistemology - how we know what we know. Huxley wants to elucidate the potential hazards of believing a concept which has not been proven correct through rigorous and logical scientific method.

➤ In stating "irrationally held truths," Huxley is referring to something that may be factually correct but the reasoning to determine this as truth was not based on evidence or rationality and cannot be justified. It can be regarded as 'blind knowledge'; for example pre-Hippocrates medicine was based only on supernatural causes of illness rather than medical observation but the likelihood is that at least some of this was factually correct.

➤ One example of something that may be considered as an irrational truth is Traditional Eastern Medicine - many of these do appear to have high efficacy despite us not knowing their mechanistic action. However, this may mean that treatment is not successful to all, and it may lead to other, untested medicines being accepted as effective. For example, homeopathy appears to 'work' on some people, although this is likely to merely be placebo and may cause danger if using it to try and cure a serious illness.

➤ If someone has wrongly reasoned something then their 'logic' or thought process is open to review and criticism by those who wish to correct it, whereas irrational truths are more resistant to criticism and therefore revision and if further research is based on this 'truth', it may encounter pitfalls further along the line.

➤ However, much of medicine does take a 'reverse engineering' route whereby we test whether a treatment is useful first, and then look to see its mechanistic action. For example, Deep Brain Stimulation is currently the best treatment for Parkinson's Disease but we still do not know how it works.

➤ Reasoned errors can often be more dangerous; in a simple maths problem, a minor calculation error leads to the wrong answer whereas a completely incorrect method may lead to the correct answer. However, if this was to determine the dosage of a drug for a patient, it is clear that we would rather have the correct answer using an incorrect method.

➤ The idea of what is rational and what is irrational constantly changes over time; Darwin's ideas were dismissed as completely irrational at the time, due to the rational explanations offered by religion. Also, many people, if they are convinced they have used a logical and rational method, will never be able to see the error of their answer/explanation.

END OF PAPER

2008

Section 1

Question 1: D

The word 'some' is key here. If we know some M are Z and all Z are T, then some M (at least the subset that were Z) are T. We cannot deduce that all M are T.

Some like to put a realistic spin on the terms to help them answer error of reasoning questions. For example, you could think of the question as 'Some A Level students take the BMAT. All taking the BMAT are applying to uni'. And we know some A Level students are applying to uni from this, but we cannot deduce that they all are.

Another useful technique here is using a Venn Diagram.

Question 2: C

Traditional evolutionary theory suggests 'animals are never altruistic' and even though there is an example given of reciprocal altruism, the conclusion is that there is 'always clear paybacks'. Thus reciprocal altruism is not truly altruistic, which is paraphrased in C. None of the other answers are consistent with this idea.

Question 3: B

There are 250 screws overall, and he can pick a 4mm screw which is 35 or 45mm long - there are 38 in total of these. $38/250 = \sim 15$

Question 4: A

The last line is the conclusion and the argument is that, as all wonder-drugs use animal testing at some stage, it is irrational to suggest this part of the study CAUSES the discovery of the drug. A logically fits with this idea, whereas the others do not.

Question 5: E

The grey die is conventional - if you rotate the dice downwards so that the 6 moves to the new position, you can see that the 5 remains in the correct place and there is a 4 opposite the 3. In the other, we must rotate the 6 sideways and downwards to its new position, and this must be in the way to ensure that the 3 and 5 in the first picture are no longer there. From these rotations we can tell that the 5 is opposite the 4, the 3 is opposite the 1 so the 2 must be opposite the 6.

Question 6: D

1 is correct because the headline suggests there is a growing digital divide, whereas the survey only found values for social networking. 2 is correct because to show a gap is growing, you also need an earlier survey. 3 is not related to the question, because it is nothing to do with the headline.

Question 7: D

$20m^2$ patio.
6 lots of 60 x 60 black tiles - $3600cm^2$ x 6 = $2.16m^2$
2 lots of 40 x 40 black tiles - $1600cm^2$ x 2 = $0.32m^2$
6 lots of 40 x 60 black tiles - $2400cm^2$ x 6 = $1.44m^2$
$2.16 + 0.32 + 1.44 = 3.92m^2$
$3.92/20 = 19.6\%$

Question 8: 39%

The relative risk was 1 for non-left handed women, and 1.39 for left-handed women. The percentage increase from 1 to 1.39 is 39%.

Question 9: B

$361 + 65 = 426$ total cases.
$153422 + 19119 = 172541$ total (estimated) person-years lived.
$426/172541 \sim 4.25/170 = 2.5\%$

~ 125 ~

Question 10: A

$144 + 20 = 164$ total cases
65245 total person-years lived.
$164/65245 \sim 1.65/65 = 2.5\%$

Question 11: D

This is the only answer which gives a potential causal reason for the positive correlation seen in the figures.
A is irrelevant as this technique is correct.
B is irrelevant to being left-handed.
C doesn't give a causal link.
E is irrelevant because the 'relative risk' value takes into account the number of people in the group, so it doesn't matter how many people are involved (unless the sample size was too small).

Question 12: A

Call the number of adults x and the ticket price y. Takings last week = xy = £1560.
40% more adults (1.4x) and 25% drop in price (0.75y)
$1.4 \times 0.75y = 1.05xy = £1638$

Question 13: E

We cannot be certain that people's opinions have necessarily been influenced by pressure groups - pressure groups are not mentioned in the argument.
2 is correct because if 34% think cars contribute more to climate change and 40% think planes, then at least some of the people are wrong.
3 is correct because if 47% think air travel should be limited but only 15% are willing to fly less often, there must be some who think air travel should be limited but are not willing to fly less often (say all 15% that are willing to fly less often also want to limit air travel, there are still 32% who follow this criteria).

Question 14: A

Steve Cram set his time in July 1985. The next date is August 1985 (S.A.), and is a quicker time, so this must have been the new WR. The next date with a quicker time is July 1995 (N.M.), so this must have been the new WR. The next date with a quicker time is July 1998 (H.E.G) and this remains the WR. So there are 3 in total.

Question 15: D

A is not necessarily correct - it may affect cell behaviour but we don't know that it will have a negative effect on health.
B is not correct - we have evidence that low level radiation does affect cell behaviour (not a 'negligible reaction').
C cannot be deduced from the passage.
D is correct - we are told that cells react to low level radiation from phones.

Question 16: D

For the first part of the tank, for every increase in measurement on the dipstick, there is an even greater volume of liquid, so we have an accelerating curve at the start - D or E. Then, for a while, the measurement of dipstick is constant relative to the volume of liquid, giving us a straight line - still D of E. Then, as the tank narrows, an increase in measurement on the dipstick means a lower increase in volume - so a decelerating curve at the end, and only D is right.

Question 17: A

Only 1 is correct - the passage argues that pop stars and celebrities shouldn't be promoting environmental awareness for various reasons, but if they have a broad appeal this suggests that they should.
2 is not correct - the idea that they are becoming more aware of themselves is irrelevant.
3 is not correct - the fact they did not gain financially has nothing to do with environmental awareness.

Question 18: A

We want to make sure that the resulting solution doesn't have more than 1% of chemical, so we must assume we have got as 'unlucky' as possible. The droplet could be as high as $0.025cm^3$ based on rounding, and the water could be as low as $5cm^3$ based on rounding. So to ensure we do not exceed 1% we can only have 2 drops - $0.05cm^3/5cm^3$.

Question 19: 79

The extension is on average 3.6 years with 30 minutes of running a day. This increase would be from 75 to 78.6, which we round up to 79.

Question 20: C

There are 3.6 years extra lifespan for running 30 minutes, and 1.4 for walking. Percentage increase is (3.6 - 1.4) x 100/1.4, which is 157%.

Question 21: C

This observation is not stated in the passage, and cannot be inferred from the passage - there is nothing about when the people started exercising. It doesn't, however, counter the passage.

Question 22: D

The conclusion is that "people who exercise regularly really do live longer," suggesting a causal link between exercising and living longer (although there may be another factor linking these 2 variables). A doesn't necessarily need to be assumed for the conclusion to make sense. The vigour of walking is not an idea of the passage, one can be overweight but still exercise a lot which counters C and E is stated.

Question 23: D

Hopefully you can see the pattern of flashes for each letter, but if not, we can just work out each flash combination (as every single one is unique), and find out how long these are. We know there is 1 flash for A and B, 2 flashes for C, D, E and F, 3 for G H I J K L M and N and 4 flashes for the rest. That makes 2 x 1 + 4 x 2 + 8 x 3 + 12 x 4 flashes which are a second each, which totals to 82 seconds. We must add 25 seconds for the gaps - 82 + 25 = 107 seconds.

Question 24: D

A is not correct because although the passage suggests the British competitors have affected their chances of winning major championships we cannot deduce that the standard of play has declined.

B cannot be inferred - although they are making a lot of money we cannot say they are more interested in this.

C cannot be assumed - although the passage suggests that the current generation are 'having lunch together' we cannot say they did not used to be on friendly terms.

D is correct - the first line of the second paragraph suggests they used to have to win many times to even make a living, whereas now they can make millions from just appearances, and we can definitely assume here that making that much money from appearances is more than you need to live.

E is not correct - we don't know whether the other commitments makes it harder to win.

Question 25: 245

Previously - r had 2.5 times more seats as b, and b had x seats, so r had 2.5x seats.

Now - If r's lead was reduced by 56, then b gained 28 reps and r lost 28. B has x + 28 and r has 2.5x - 28.

R now has 1.5 times more seats than b, so 2.5x - 28 = 1.5 (x+28).

x =70.

So number of seats - 2.5 x + x = 245.

Question 26: D

1 is correct, because the argument suggests that only those who have committed crimes before should have their DNA kept, because only these people will commit sexual and violent crimes. However, they could be first time offenders.

2 is correct because those who are not found guilty may have committed a crime and then they are not first time offenders, and should have their DNA sample kept according to the author's logic.

3 is not correct - solving sexual and violent crime without DNA evidence is irrelevant to this particular argument.

Question 27: C

Let's call the convoy's speed x and the courier's speed y. Then use distance = speed x time.

Time to get from the front to the back = 1/120 hours, and to get here we can add the speeds of the convoy and courier to get the net speed of him travelling backwards. 1km = (1/120)(x+y), so x + y = 120

Time to get from the back to the front = 1/20 hours, and to get there we have the find the difference between the speed of the courier and the convoy to get the net speed of him travelling forwards. 1km = (1/20)(y-x), so y - x = 20.

Solve simultaneous equations x+y=120 and y-x=20 and we find y = 70.

Question 28: E

All answers are correct. The 3rd sentence assumes point 1 - that increased climate change will cause increased flooding. The last sentence assumes point 2 - that there will be limited geographic mobility due to flooding, which assumes there will be no action taken to prevent this flooding. Point 3 is correct because the argument suggests people in flooded areas will find it even more difficult to sell their houses

Question 29: C

Test the combination of numbers it could be - we know there is only 1 correct combination. For example, the 7s must either be the second digit of a number or just be a 7. We also know that numbers cannot be repeated. Hopefully you should get that the combination is 34 37 4 27 33 7, so the highest number is 37.

Question 30: E

1 is correct - just because there is another more common cause of accidents it doesn't mean that these speed traps are not of use. 2 is not correct - the fact still remains that drivers under 25 cause more accidents than drivers who speed. 3 is correct - the last sentence suggests safe and responsible driving doesn't include obeying the speed limit.

Question 31: B

Visualisation - 1 way to do this is to draw a 3D grid that is 3 x 2 x 2, see which parts of the grid that piece F and G would cover, and you should see that the only piece to fit in would be B.

Question 32: D

Average of 14 cycle trips per person per year, which is 1% of their trips. Thus there are 1400 trips per person per year, which is roughly 1400/50 ~ 27 per week.

Question 33: D

A is not correct - we know 85% cycle less than once a week, but we don't know what distance. B cannot be inferred - there is not enough info.

C cannot be inferred - not enough info. D can be inferred - 15% cycle at least once a week, 8% at least once a month, and 69% less than once a year. This leaves 100 - 8 - 15 - 69 = 8% that cycle between 1 and 11 times a year.

Question 34: C

The graph suggests that having more cars means you cycle less. The text suggests that having more income means you cycle more. Thus we need a reason to explain the inverse relation of income and cars. C is the only one that does this.

Question 35: B

1 is not correct. Males between 21 and 29 cycle 78 miles a year, making 27 trips, so $78/27 \sim 2.6$ miles per trip. Males between 11 and 16 cycle 74 miles a year, making 46 trips, so $74/46 \sim 1.5$ miles per trip. The first result is less than double the second.

2 is correct. We can see that males between 11 and 16 cycle 46 times a year and males between 17 to 20 cycle 29 times a year, so the former cycle more often. However, they average less per trip ($74/46 \sim 1.5$ miles, $59/29 \sim 2$ miles per trip).

END OF SECTION

Section 2

Question 1: D

D is the only answer where there is a negative concentration gradient. E, the loss of urine occurs as a result of changes in pressure. All the others have a positive concentration gradient so could occur by diffusion alone.

Question 2: C

Y^{3-} has gained 3 electrons to have a configuration of 2, 8, 8. So it usually has a configuration of 2, 8, 5, meaning it is in group 5. Since it has 3 electron shells, it is in period 3.

Question 3: B

The amount of Y must increase over time because X decays into Y so. Since there is 100 Y at the end every graph, the correct graph will show a mass of 50 at 20 seconds.

Question 4: D

$P = 2 \ (3x10^{-3})^2 x \ (2.5 \ x \ 10^4)$

$P = 9 \ x \ 10^{-6} x \ 5 \ x \ 10^4$

$P = 45 \ x \ 10^{-2}$

$P = 4.5 \ x \ 10^{-1}$

Question 5: C

Let **a** be the recessive allele and A be the dominant allele. Crossing two heterozygotes gives:

	A	**a**
A	AA $(\frac{1}{3})$	Aa $(\frac{1}{3})$
a	Aa $(\frac{1}{3})$	aa (dead)

Proportion of the live offspring which are homozygous dominant $= \frac{1}{3}$

Question 6: E

The quickest way to do this is by setting up algebraic equations:

If you're unsure how to do this then check out the chemistry chapter in *The Ultimate BMAT Guide.*

For Chlorine: $B = 3A + 2Y$

A. $8 \neq 3 + 6$
B. $8 \neq 3 + 8$
C. $4 \neq 3 + 6$
D. $16 \neq 6 + 12$
E. $16 = 6 + 10$

E is the answer since it is the only option that satisfies $B = 3A + 2Y$.

Question 7: B

$$= (n + 1)^{th} \; term - n^{th} \; term$$

$$= \frac{n+1}{n+2} - \frac{n}{n+1}$$

$$= \frac{n+1(n+1)-n(n+2)}{(n+2)(n+1)}$$

$$= \frac{n^2 + 2n+1-n^2-2n}{(n+2)(n+1)}$$

$$= \frac{1}{(n+2)(n+1)}$$

Question 8: A

Height lifted $= 0.4 \; x \; 5 \; = \; 2 \; m$
$Gravitational \; Potential \; Energy \; = \; mg\Delta h \; = \; 100 \; x \; 10 \; x \; 2 \; = \; 2,000 \; J$
The tension in the cable $= \; weight \; = \; mg$
$= 10 \; x \; 100 \; = \; 1,000 N$
The load does not accelerate as the crane lifts the load at a constant speed.

Question 9: D

Between 0 and 11 seconds the oxygen demand exceeds the oxygen supply. When this happens, the muscle cells use the oxygen that is available for aerobic respiration, but must gain the extra energy required from anaerobic respiration, so both occur.

Question 10: C

C_6H_{16} is not a plausible product - even if a 6 carbon atom molecule was fully saturated it would have 14 hydrogens (not 16!).

Question 11: D

A beta particle is emitted from the nucleus of an atom when a neutron changes to a proton and electron. Thus, the mass number is unchanged but the atomic number increases by 1.

Question 12: E

> Lipids break down to form glycerol and fatty acids - the acid would lower the pH.
> Proteins break down to form amino acids - the acid would lower the pH.
> Carbohydrates break down into sugars like glucose - this doesn't affect the pH.

Question 13: D

Triangle LMN can be rotated about the origin 90 degrees to give triangle PQR. Thus, a further 270 degree rotation will reverse this transformation. This can be accomplished by 2 and then 5.

Question 14: D

This tests your understanding of Le Chatelier's principle. Adding a catalyst does not affect the equilibrium. Adding nitrogen won't have an effect either as it is not involved in the reaction. Changing pressure will have no effect as there are the same number of moles of gas on each side of the equation. Decreasing the temperature will favour the exothermic reactions, so this would shift the equilibrium to the right- resulting in more CO being removed.

Question 15: F

Z is the car's weight because it is constant; Kinetic energy would increase until the terminal velocity was reached. Y is velocity or drag force, which increases as the car increases in speed. X can be acceleration or resultant force - this starts high but decreases to zero as terminal velocity is reached. The only possible combination that satisfies these is F.

Question 16: A

$$Area = \frac{1}{2} \times base \times height$$

$$= \frac{1}{2} \times \left(4 - \sqrt{6}\right) \times \left(6 + \sqrt{6}\right)$$

$$= \frac{24 + 4\sqrt{6} - 6\sqrt{6} - 6}{2}$$

$$= \frac{18 - 2\sqrt{6}}{2}$$

$$= 9 - \sqrt{6}$$

Question 17: B

Neural responses require a stimulus to be detected by a receptor. This sends an impulse via a sensory neuron to the CNS which then sends impulses via motor neuron to cause muscles to contract/relax to bring about the response. Thus, the correct order is represented by option B.

Question 18: F θ

Comparing an alkane and an amide from the given information, we remove 1 hydrogen atom from the alkane but add 1 Carbon, 1 Oxygen, 1 Nitrogen and 2 Hydrogen. Thus, there is a net addition of 1C 1O 1N and 1H. Add this to the alkane formula: $C_nH_{2n+2} + CONH = C_{n+1}H_{2n+3}ON$

Question 19: C

This is a tricky question that becomes much easier once you've draw a diagram. Remember that a bearing is the clockwise angle from the due North position.

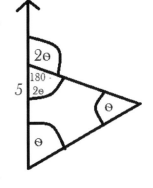

Since the bearing after walking 5km is 2ɵ; the acute angle in the triangle must be 180 - 2ɵ. Therefore, the third angle is ɵ.

Since the triangle has two identical angles – it is an isosceles triangle:

We need to find **x**:

Splitting the triangle into two right angles:

$$cos\ ɵ = \frac{Adjacent}{Hypotenuse} = \frac{0.5x}{5}$$

$5\ cos\ ɵ = 0.5x$

$x = 10\ cos\ ɵ$

Question 20: F

With the switch closed, all current will avoid resistor Y and flow in the branch with the switch because it is the path of least resistance. Thus, the 12V will be split evenly between resistors X and Z.

When the switch was open: $V = IR;\ 12 = 20mA\ x\ R$

Thus, $R = \frac{12}{20x10^{-3}} = 0.6\ x\ 10^3\ \Omega$

Each resistor therefore has a resistance of $0.2\ x\ 10^3\ \Omega$

When the switch is closed; $V = I\ x\ 2R; 12 = I\ x\ 2\ x\ 0.2\ x\ 10^3$

$I = \frac{12}{0.4\ x\ 10^3}$

$= 30\ x\ 10^{-3} = 30\ mA$

Question 21: B

1. Correct - in a double circulation, one complete circuit means that blood goes through the heart twice i.e. Lungs → Left Side of Heart → Body → Right Side of Heat→ Lungs
2. Incorrect- The lungs receive 100% of the cardiac output but since the left side of the heart pumps blood to the whole body, the kidneys + liver don't receive 100% of cardiac output.
3. Correct- all of the blood from the liver will eventually reach the lungs.
4. Incorrect- the liver has a dual blood supply.

Question 22: D

A. False- there are strong covalent bonds between all the atoms.
B. False- in graphite – a carbon atom is only bonded to 3 other Carbon atoms.
C. False- graphite conducts electricity and is soft but diamond doesn't conduct electricity and is very hard.
D. True- you might have known this or arrived at the answer via a process of elimination.
E. False- graphite is an electrical conductor.

Question 23: C

The work done by the braking force is equal to the kinetic energy of the lorry $Work\ Done = E_k$;

$$Force\ x\ Distance = \frac{mv^2}{2}$$

Thus, $Distance = \frac{mv^2}{2F}$

Question 24: A

Since the solutions are a & b; this can be shown as: $(x - a)(x - b) = 0$

➤ $x^2 - ax - bx + ab = 0$
➤ *Since $ab = 3$; $x^2 - x(a - b) + 3 = 0$*
➤ *Since $a - b = -5$; $x^2 - x(-5) + 3 = 0$*
➤ *Simplify to give: $x^2 + 5x + 3 = 0$*

Question 25: D

The man received the Y allele from his father, and got the colour blindness X allele from his mother, so she must carry the recessive allele. The man must pass on this X allele if he has a daughter, as he only has the one recessive X allele.

Question 26: C

Using n=cV; Moles of Sulphuric acid = $12.5 \; x \; 10^{-3} \; x \; 2 = 0.025 \; moles$

The molar ratio between **XOH** and Sulphuric acid is 2:1 so there were 0.05 moles of **XOH** that reacted.

A_r of **XOH** $= \frac{2.8}{0.05} = 56$

A_r of **X** = A_r of **XOH** - A_r of OH

$= 56 - 16 - 1$

$= 39$

Question 27: C

Time taken for sound to travel via air $= t$

Time taken for sound to travel via steel $= t + 1.5$

Speed of sound in air $= 300 \, m/s$

Speed of sound in steel $= 4800 m/s$

Distance travelled by sound in air = Distance travelled by sound in steel

$300 \; x \; (t + 1.5) = 4800 \; x \; t$

$300t + 450 = 4800t$

$4500t = 450; T = 0.1$

Distance of train $= 4800 \; x \; 0.1 = 480m$

END OF SECTION

Section 3

When you can measure what you are speaking about, and express it in numbers, you know something about it; but when you cannot ... your knowledge is of a meagre and unsatisfactory kind.

➢ Through this quote, Lord Kelvin argues that scientific quality depends on quantification, suggesting that the expression of unquantified knowledge is inadequate.

➢ This concept can be applied to almost anything in life; for example, how can we know and understand what makes a business successful if we cannot express their business performance numerically?

➢ Regarding science and medicine specifically, the majority of scientific method requires the quantification of the link between the independent variable and the dependent variable. We also regularly need to use statistical techniques to see if there is a statistically significant difference between our control and what we are testing, and this is vital to maintain safe practice and minimising errors. For example, in a clinical trial, the treatment in question is tested against a placebo and it is only confirmed as effective if there is a statistically significant difference between the efficacy of each treatment.

➢ However, we often cannot quantify our findings in medicine, such as for psychiatric illnesses. For example, patients with bipolar disorder cannot be diagnosed using simple scientific method as patients are on a spectrum. Instead, psychoanalysis is used and there is very little quantification involved. Numerical scales that are used for diagnosis are regularly criticised and there is never an agreed consensus on how to use them.

➢ Quantification also often ignores the concept of individual differences.

Life has a natural end, and doctors and others caring for a patient need to recognise that the point may come in the progression of a patient's condition where death is drawing near.

➤ This statement suggests that awareness of the end of natural life is important, and that prolonging the dying process should not occur without regard for the patient's wishes.

➤ This guidance is important when considering whether to withhold or withdraw treatment. To ensure the best care, considerations must include the patient's desires, medical indications, benefits and burdens of treatment and quality of life that may result from the treatment.

➤ One could suggest that this is support for passive euthanasia, and/or DNRs. If there is no benefit to the patient or the benefits are outweighed by the burdens, we may decide to prevent patients suffering needlessly. The risks and consequences of not recognising this is the prolonged pain and distress someone may experience if they are kept on life support.

➤ Other factors to consider: the dilemmas patients, families and doctors face when considering modern techniques to prolong life, whether there is hope of recovery, all the difficult ethical and legal issues.

Science is the great antidote to the poison of enthusiasm and superstition.

➢ This statement relates to the objectivity of scientific method, whereby we remain unbiased and develop conclusions true to our results rather than true to our beliefs. This is the opposite of what enthusiasm and superstition is regularly based on - subjectivity.

➢ Science, by definition, is completely free of any emotion, ego or enthusiasm. Scientists should deal with everything in a logical, rational manner.

➢ Enthusiasm and superstition often cloud this rational scientific judgement, and thus science's job is to keep humanity sane. Humans are enthusiastic and emotional creatures, and superstitions flow naturally when emotion meets unrestricted intelligence. This has led to situations such as witch hunts and, notions that have later been dismissed through science.

➢ Generally, enthusiasm and superstition are based on untested and unconfirmed hypotheses. We can thence regard science as the antidote because we can use it to test whether this enthusiasm and superstition is based on rationality, or whether there is no basis. Through science, we attempt to see whether there is causality between a change in the independent variable and a change in the dependent variable, ensuring there are no confounding factors.

➢ Science is based upon accuracy and precision, whereas enthusiasm and superstition are the 'poisons' which are based on the opposite.

END OF PAPER

2009

Section 1

Question 1: 15

35 Monarchs reigned for less than 40 years, and 20 monarchs reigned for less than 20 years, so 35-20 = 15 monarchs reigned for 20-40 years.

Question 2: B

The final paragraph suggests childbirth is either done away from the labour ward **OR** surrounded by the as much pain relief an medical intervention as possible, which suggests that this level of relief/intervention is not available away from a labour ward.

A is not correct as the issue does not imply that the Health Secretary was either right or wrong; it instead just outlines what they believe.

C cannot be implied from the information we are given.

D is incorrect as the words 'strongly opposed' are far too strong relative to saying 'the delivery of babies has shifted too far in favour of medicalisation'

E is not correct as the passage doesn't mention the progression of mothers/babies/

Question 3:D

We must select each graph in turn, and see if each other graph has 2 bars at the wrong height.

Starting with A, we can see that there are 2 bars incorrect relative to B, but 3 relative to C, so A or C cannot be right.

If we check with B, then A, B and D have 2 bars the incorrect height but E has 4 bars at a different height, so B or E cannot be correct.

This leaves D, and checking this shows that all bars have 2 incorrect bars relative to D.

Question 4: B

The conclusion, highlighted by the use 'Given that,' is 'the high cost of investing in preventative measures would be unreasonable.' This is paraphrased in B.

A is evidence for the conclusion above rather than the conclusion itself. C also relates to background information/evidence in the text, which actually suggests the opposite of this statement. D suggests the opposite of the conclusion.

E is not correct because although the argument suggests billions of pounds were lost, it doesn't say whether the government should compensate for this.

Question 5: E

There is at least 1 birthday per month - at least 12 birthdays. There are 3 pairs of twins with birthdays in April - at least 6 in April. There are at least 2 pairs of twins with birthdays in other months - 2 more birthdays not in April.

At least 13 birthdays not in April + 6 in April = at least 19 birthdays. There are exactly double granddaughters as grandsons, so we cannot make 19 or 20 with this information. The minimum is thus 21 (14 granddaughters and 7 grandsons).

Question 6: G

All answers are correct.

1 is correct because the argument suggests campaigns are not needed because there are only a few deaths caused by ecstasy a year, but this may increase if the campaigns were not present.

2 is correct because the author concludes that ecstasy is not as dangerous as many people believe, but this is only mentioned relative to horse riding.

3 is correct because the author only talks about the number of deaths per year caused by each activity, rather than the rate.

Question 7: C

Gold and silver would cost the same, so if we call x the number of times equipment is used in the year, £80 + x = £100 + 0.5x so x=40 - the membership would cost £120 with this option. With bronze, it would cost 70 + 3x40 = £190, so changing saves £190 - £120 = £70.

Question 8: B

421 did not report a crime, and 133 of these thought it was insufficiently important. Thus 133/421 is the probability, and we want to find out what this is in decimals. One way of doing this is realising 133 x 3 = 399 so it is less than 0.33, but 133 x 4 = 532 so it is more than 0.25.

Question 9: G

None are correct.
1 is not right because we cannot infer any information about next year from this data.
2 is not correct because we know nothing about the attitudes of those that didn't experience or witness crime.
3 is not correct because we have no idea about the overlap of people's responses.

Question 10: A

We are given general attitudes to why people didn't report crime in the text, and a common reason is people lacking confidence in the police, which is suggested in A. Particular areas of London, drugs, crime against criminals and paperwork are not implied in the text.

Question 11: D

This can fold twice to make the shape given. Cut the shape out and try folding it if you struggle to visualise. Folding A would mean the opposite only one set of adjacent corners match. Folding B or C produces a shape similar to A, which cannot then fold to form a triangle.

Question 12: B

The conclusion is 'the government should act now to protect people...and make slimming pills subject to the same strict controls as medicines.' This statement suggests the government is already introducing legislation, weakening the argument that the government need to act now. The other answers do not link to this conclusion.

Question 13: E

Test each combination.
A is possible. For example, if the right bag has half green and half red already, then one red is added and one red is taken away.
B is possible with the same example as A.
C is possible. For example, if the right bag has two greens, one red is added and one green is removed.
D is possible with the same example as A.
E is not possible as it will not be possible to have half green and half red in the right bag if it has more than two marbles and only starts with one colour.

F is possible with the same example as C.

Question 14: A

The conclusion is that 'Colour psychology...improving the success of interrogation.' The evidence is that the colours given put people more at ease. To link the evidence and conclusion, it must be assumed that interrogation is more successful if people are more at ease. The other statements do not have to be assumed for the argument to hold.

Question 15: D

There are 7 squares which fulfil the criteria, but some cannot be used in combination with each other.
Squares - 3 between MD and OA, one 2 spaces left of AD, one 2 above JS, one 2 above NT and another to the right of this.

Question 16: s: 38, b: 36

We know USA had 36 golds and 110 medals in total, so 74 = silver + bronze medals. Based on the weighting where gold is worth 3, we know 112 = 2silver + bronze. Solving these simultaneous equation gives s = 38 and b = 36.

Question 17: 13

Germany won 16 golds, so the max Australia could have is 15. G + S + B = 46 and 3G + 2S + B = 89. Taking the first from the second gives 2G + S = 43. Since G = 15 to minimise S we get 30 + S = 43. Therefore S = 13.

Question 18: B

China have 51/100, USA have 36/110, Russia have 23/72 and GB have 19/47. China is the only above ½ and Russia and USA are under 1/3. GB have between 1/3 and ½ and are thus second.

Question 19: F

1 could be correct - 3 golds and 5 silvers gives a score of 19, and divided by 4.6 (population) gives a medal weighting per million population of roughly 4.5.
2 cannot be correct - even if all of them were bronze, giving a score of 3, this would give a medal weighting per million population of 10.
3 can be correct - Slovenia have a total weighted score of 9, which could be achieved by 1 gold, 1 silver and 4 bronzes.

Question 20: C

Both are correct. GBs weighted score is 98, and 98/62 is greater than 220/142 but less than 2.5. Russia would have 139/142, which is under 1.

Question 21: 50g

The drinks are 1.5J in 200ml 2J in 400ml. With 300ml of the second drink we would have 1.5J and with 200ml of the first drink we have another 1.5J, giving 3J in total. We need 4J overall, so we need 1J extra. The supplement has 2J per 100g, so we need 50g for 1J.

Question 22: A

1 is assumed in the second to last line 'the recipient knows to be appropriate.'
2 is assumed in the last line 'only given to the extent that it is deserved.'
3 and 4 are not assumed.

Question 23: E

Month 124 is a September. From this, we can work out that month 254 is a July, 264 is a May, 274 is a March, 284 is a January and 294 is a November. November does not have a 31st day of the month so the last option is not possible.

Question 24: E

None are correct.
1 We don't know anything about sexual activity of those who do and don't drink, only pregnancy rates.
2 We cannot infer this from the statistic alone.
3 We do not know how many girls have consumed alcohol by age 16, only the 40% of pregnant teenage girls below 16 were under the influence of alcohol.

Question 25: A

Trial and error to see if the data fits. Don't try and work out exact proportions, just test if the higher and lower values are in the correct place.

Question 26: E

The passage describes that ants regularly 'talk' in their nests and give an example of this aiding in the survival of blue butterflies. A is not correct as it is not suggested that ants 'talking' will actually harm their survival as a species (although it will maybe harm individuals). B is not correct because the blue butterfly story given is just an example. C is not correct because the slaughtering talked about is not intentional. D is not correct because we cannot deduce that the ability to talk arose due to the threat from parasites.

Question 27: B

Tokens needed for a free meal must be over 7 otherwise Tim would not run out. If this is 8, then he will lose a token a day and he will have a while until this runs out. If this is 9, then he will lose 2 tokens a day and this would leave him with 8 tokens on Tuesday 9th. Then drawing a table is useful from here - he will have 15 tokens on Wednesday morning, and he will have 7 tokens on the Tuesday after this, which would mean no free meal.

Question 28: B

The conclusion is the last sentence: 'if the Kepler telescope finds that such planets exist, we can at last be confident that there is life on planets other than Earth', and the evidence is that the Kepler telescope can find Earth sized planets in the 'habitable zone'. The assumption to link this evidence and conclusion is that Earth sized planets in the zone = life existing.

Question 29: D

Going from left to right:
- ➤ 1 is unique.
- ➤ 2, 6 and 8 are the same.
- ➤ 3, 5 and 7 are the same.
- ➤ 4 is unique.
- ➤ 9 and 10 are the same.
- ➤ 11 is unique.
- ➤ 12 is unique.
- ➤ Hence there are 7 different patterns.

Question 30: D

The conclusion is the last sentence: 'the more systematic and organised...the more likely they will produced valid explanations,' suggesting common sense explanations are less likely to be valid than those by scientific method.

Question 31: D

The lift will begin to move to 10 (equal distance to 4, but more requests going up than down). It will then go back to 7, to 4, to 0, to 14, then to 16. This means there will be 5 stops **BEFORE** it reaches 16 - make sure you do not include the stop for 16.

Question 32: C

Cattle, wool and pigs show a decrease, potatoes go from 81.2 to 117.1 and vegetables go from 34.5 to 38.3. Hopefully you can easily see that the former percentage increase is larger than the latter.

Question 33: C

There is an first an increase between 1994 to 1995, then a slight decrease to 1996, then a bigger decrease to 1997 and another decrease to 1998. The only sector that shows this out of the answers given is Livestock.

Question 34: D

This is the correct answer. In 1998, the prices of commodities being exported decreased. From 1997 to 1998 there was a decrease in farm crop £ output but quite a large increase for horticulture, suggesting that this decrease in price affected the farm crop commodities more, presumably because more were exported. The line 'if volumes of production have not changed' is key here otherwise we would not be able to infer this.

A cannot be safely inferred as, even if we know the changes in £ output, we do not know what farmers may have changed to and from. The £ output of vegetables increased more than flowers anyway.

B is not correct - from 1995 to 1996, the £ output of cattle decreased and the output of pigs increased. Anyway, we do not have any information about the price of pigs and cattle, only their £ output (it could have also been affected by the absolute amount bought)
C cannot be inferred - although the income was higher in 1998 than 1980, this may not necessarily been to do with the strength of the pound. Many other factors could have caused this e.g. a flood or a drought.
E cannot be assumed from this data alone; we do not know how other factors (such as volume of production) have influenced the £ output.

Question 35: E

The percentage change in sheep from 1997 to 1998 is (237.4 - 245.1)/245.1 = ~1/30 ~3.3%.

All the sheep that are not exported are the same value as before, whereas all the sheep that were exported lost 5% value. If there was a 3.3% drop in value because of a 5% drop in value of those exported, 3.3/5 = 66% is the percentage of sheep exported.

END OF SECTION

Section 2

Question 1: C

Since is homozygous dominant and B is homozygous recessive, D must be heterozygous. If E is homozygous recessive then there is a 50:50 chance for F to be homozygous recessive and heterozygous. If E is heterozygous there is a 25:50:25 chance for F to be homozygous dominant, heterozygous and homozygous recessive.

Question 2: E

Only molecules with a double bond can take part in polymerisation. If there is one double bond, there are double the number of other atoms to carbon e.g. $C_{24}H_{48}$. CHI_3 and C_3H_7Br don't contain a double bond.

Question 3: C

$$Using\ F = ma;\ a = \frac{900-600}{60}$$

Thus $a = \frac{300}{60} = 5\ ms^{-2}$

The resultant force is upwards (900-600), thus the direction of acceleration is upwards.

Question 4: C

The probability of picking a red ball $= \frac{x}{x+y+z}$

The probability of picking a blue ball $= \frac{y}{x+y+z}$.

Since the first ball is replaced, the probability of picking a red ball and then a blue ball $= = \frac{x}{x+y+z} \times \frac{y}{x+y+z} = \frac{xy}{(x+y+z)^2}$

Question 5: E

A. Clones don't always have the same phenotype due to environmental factors.
B. Twins aren't always members of a clone – they can be non-identical.
C. Clones can occur naturally.
D. Mutations result in variation – not clones.
E. Correct - clones contain identical DNA.

Question 6: B

This is a simple recall question- SiO_2 is the only structure that forms a giant molecular structure.

Question 7: E

Recall that $P = IV$; $V = \frac{P}{I} = Watt\ per\ Amp.$

The other units are not equivalent to a volt.

Question 8: B

Solving this requires you to use Pythagoras' theorem twice.

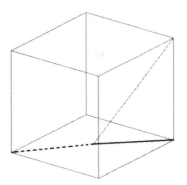

First, we need to find the length of the added solid line which is half the length of a diagonal joining the two bottom corners. This is given by: $\sqrt{1^2 + 1^2} = \sqrt{2}$

Since the solid line is only half the length of the diagonal, its length $= \frac{\sqrt{2}}{2}$

Thus, the length of the original line is given by: $x^2 = \left(\frac{\sqrt{2}}{2}\right)^2 + 1^2 = \frac{2}{4} + 1$

Thus, $x^2 = \frac{6}{4} = \frac{3}{2}$; $x = \sqrt{\frac{3}{2}}$

~ 155 ~

Question 9: D

A. Correct because an increased number of alleles always increases the risk.
B. Correct because increased alcohol intake increases risk regardless of the allele number.
C. Correct as drinking increases the risk more than allele number.
D. Incorrect because there is an increased risk from drinking alcohol (risk value of 1.0 to 4.0 for 0 alleles) than from increased allele numbers (1.0 to 1.5 to 1.8).
E. Correct as the risk is increased more with 2 mutant alleles for heavy drinkers than for light drinkers.

Question 10: E

A_r of $CO_2 = 12 + (2 \times 16) = 44$

Number of moles of $CO_2 = \frac{4.77}{44} \approx 0.1 \; moles$

Since the molar ratio is 1:1, there must be 0.1 moles of Carbon in the original compound.

Mass of Carbon in original compound $= 0.1 \times 12 = 1.2 \; g$

Thus, the percentage of carbon in original compound $= \frac{1.2}{2} = 60\%$

E is the closest answer to this (note that we underestimated in the original calculations to make the maths easier so the final value is lower than the actual answer). Make sure you check the options first to see how much margin you have to round numbers.

Question 11: C

This is beta radiation because the radiation reaches a detector 30 cm away but not one 1 m away. Alpha radiation would not reach either detector.

The initial count rate is 220 and falls to 20 (= background radiation) over time. Thus, the radioactive source initially results in 200 counts/min. Thus, the half life is when the count rate decreases to $\frac{200}{2} + 20 = 120$. The time for this is at 2.40 hours.

Question 12: C

Do the calculation in brackets first, which is $\frac{2^3}{3} = \frac{8}{3}$

The next step is: $\frac{\left(\frac{8}{3}\right)^2}{2} = \frac{\frac{64}{9}}{2}$

$\frac{64}{18} = \frac{32}{9}$

Question 13: B

This is a tricky question as you can easily over interpret it depending on your level of knowledge. You need to identify which process will be severely impacted in hypoxia (low blood oxygen).

➤   A: In short, a low blood O_2 concentration won't cause a severe disruption in CO_2 diffusion. In fact, hypoxia will facilitate CO_2 to leave the blood at the alveoli via the Haldane effect (which you are not expected to know about for the BMAT!).

➤   B: Glucose absorption in the gut is an active process and would therefore require ATP derived from aerobic respiration which is dependent on oxygen. Thus, hypoxia would impair this.

➤   C: Hypoxia would increase the concentration gradient so oxygen would leave the alveoli even more quickly.

➤   D, E and F: These are just passive processes so unlikely to be impacted **immediately and severely** in hypoxia.

~ 157 ~

Question 14: B

A more reactive element can displace a less reactive element in a compound. This happens in 2, 3 and 4. In 1, 5 and 6 a less reactive element displaces a more reactive element which is not possible.

Question 15: D

The distance travelled is the area under the graph. Convert the x axis into seconds when calculating.

Distance travelled in the first minute $= 15 \, x \, 60 \, + \, 5 \, x \, 6 \, x \frac{1}{2}$

$= \, 900 \, + \, 150 \, = \, 1050 m$

Distance travelled between 1 and 4 minutes $= \, 20 \, x \, 3 \, x \, 60 \, = \, 3600 \, m$

Assume the curve between 4 and 7 minutes is a triangle to calculate the distance: $20 \, x \, 3 \, x \, 60 \, x \frac{1}{2} = 1800 m$

Total Distance travelled $= 1050 + 3600 + 1800$

$= 6450m = 6.45$ km

This is an overestimate since the last part of the journey is < 1800 m.

Thus, the answer must be less than 6.45 km: D – 6 km.

Question 16: F

$$\sqrt{\frac{2 \, x \, 10^3 + 8 \, x 10^2}{\frac{1}{2500} + 3 \, x \, 10^{-4}}}$$

$$= \sqrt{\frac{2800}{\frac{4}{10000} + \frac{3}{10000}}}$$

$$= \sqrt{\frac{2800}{\frac{7}{10^4}}}$$

$$= \sqrt{\frac{2800 \, x \, 10^4}{7}}$$

$$= \sqrt{400 \, x \, 10^4} \, = \sqrt{4 \, x \, 10^6}$$

$$= 2 \, x \, 10^3 = 2000$$

Question 17: F
All of the statements are correct – competition can be both between species (inter-specific) and between members of the same species (intra-specific). Natural selection can lead to both evolution and extinction.

Question 18: D

This is actually trickier than it first appears and it's easy to get bogged down in it. The best way is to form simultaneous equations and solve algebraically. If you're unfamiliar with this approach then see the chemistry chapter in *The Ultimate BMAT Guide*.

$$For\ Hydrogen: B\ =\ 2C$$
$$For\ Nitrogen: B\ =\ 2A\ +\ 2$$
$$For\ Oxygen: 3B\ =\ 6A\ +\ C\ +\ 2$$
$$Thus, 2C\ =\ 2A\ +\ 2\ ;\ C\ =\ A\ +\ 1$$
$$3B\ =\ 3(2A\ +\ 2)\ =\ 6A\ +\ 6$$
$$Thus, 6A\ +\ 6\ =\ 6A\ +\ C\ +\ 2$$
$$Simplify\ to\ give: C\ =\ 4$$
$$Since\ B\ =\ 2C\ =\ 8$$

Question 19: B

Gravitational potential energy at top = Kinetic energy at bottom

$$E_k = \frac{mv^2}{2} = \frac{5\ x\ 20^2}{2}$$
$$= \frac{5\ x\ 400}{2} = 1,000\ J$$
$$E_p = mg\Delta h = 5\ x\ 10\ x\ h$$
$$50\ h = 1000;\ h\ =\ 20m$$

Question 20: D

$Volume\ of\ Sphere\ = \frac{4\pi r^3}{3}$

$Volume\ of\ cylinder\ = \pi r^2 h$

$In\ this\ case, h\ =\ 2r\ so\ \pi r^2 h\ =\ 2\pi r^3$

Fraction of volume occupied by sphere $= \frac{4\pi r^3}{3} \div 2\pi r^3 = \frac{4}{6} = \frac{2}{3}$

Question 21: D

The oxygen in the alveolus is from inspired air so is high, whereas the blood in the capillary is deoxygenated. The carbon dioxide is high in the capillary after respiration whereas it is low in inspired air.

Question 22: D

No bonds are broken in 2 or 3 - bonds are only made. In reaction 1, H-H and I-I bonds are broken and in 4, the C-Br bond is broken.

Question 23: A

The weight of the system is 20,000 + 5,000 + 5,000 = 30,000 kg.

$Using\ F\ =\ ma;\ a\ = \frac{15,000}{30,000} =\ 0.5 ms^{-2}$

To find T; apply F= ma to the individual carriage = $5000\ x\ 0.5\ =\ 2500\ N$

Question 24: A

$$y = 5\left(\frac{x}{2} - 3\right)^2 - 10$$

$$\frac{y+10}{5} = \left(\frac{x}{2} - 3\right)^2$$

$$\sqrt{\frac{y+10}{5}} = \frac{x}{2} - 3$$

$$\frac{x}{2} = 3 + \sqrt{\frac{y+10}{5}}$$

$$x = 6 + 2\sqrt{\frac{y+10}{5}}$$

Question 25: F

1. Insulin controls blood glucose levels, not water content (that is ADH).
2. Homeostasis depends on the hormonal and nervous systems.
3. Statements 3, 4 and 5 are correct.

Question 26: C

M_r of CH_2 = 12 + 2= 14

Thus, BrCl must have an M_r of 114 to make up 128.

This is only possible if the Cl is 35 and the Br is 79.

Since Cl^{35} is three times as common as Cl^{37}; 75% of CH_2BrCl will be Cl^{35}

Since Br^{79} is equally as common as Br^{81}; 50% of CH_2BrCl will be Br^{79}

Therefore, $\frac{3}{4}x\frac{1}{2} = \frac{3}{8}$ of CH_2BrCl will have a mass of 128.

Question 27: E

➢   The first graph shows 2 cycles of the wave taking 60m.
   o   Thus, the wavelength = 30 m
➢   The second graph shows 3 complete cycles taking 0.6s.
   o   Thus, the frequency = $\frac{3}{0.6} = 5$

$Wave\ speed\ =\ wavelength\ x\ frequency\ =\ 30\ x\ 5\ =\ 150\ ms^{-1}$

END OF SECTION

~ 161 ~

Section 3

You must be honest and open and act with integrity.

➤ The statement argues that a good doctor is one that discloses all information to patients without exception, and builds a relationship based upon complete sincerity and integrity.

➤ These are vital attributes for a doctor to have and are highlighted in the Good Medical Practice booklet given out by the GMC. Full disclosure allows a patient to make an informed decision about their health and allows the expression of true autonomy. Furthermore, these qualities are likely to make the patient feel more at ease relative to a dishonest, closed doctor.

➤ However, of course full disclosure can often be undesirable. For example, if a doctor is running some tests for the presence of a disease, and it comes back positive, this should be run again before the patient is informed (Bayes Theorem explains that in many of these situations, a false positive can be more likely than a true positive). False positives can lead to unnecessary stress and worry. The neurologist Oliver Sacks describes in his books that he sometimes decided not to tell patients with cognitive impairments about their disorder so that they could at least attempt to have a good quality of life despite their incurable condition.

➤ This question can also be approached from the angle of prima facie principles and patient confidentiality. Of course, if a patient present you with obvious signs of self-harm, or confides in you that they have stolen drugs in order to overdose, then you clearly have an responsibility to inform your seniors and break the trust. Other examples of breaking confidentiality include when other people's health may be at risk - HIV positive patient intending to have unprotected sex or a patient threatening to maim someone after their discharge.

➤ A doctor should obviously strive to have these attributes but what is most important is the best health of the patient and this should never be compromised.

Science is a way of trying not to fool yourself.

➤ Fooling oneself is convincing oneself that a particular belief, observation or opinion is the truth when it is actually false. The empirical nature of science means that falsehoods can be avoided and it develops concrete evidence for us to base theories on.

➤ Scientists must be objective - the ability to remain unbiased and develop conclusions true to our results rather than true to our beliefs.

➤ There are many examples of where passion and bias have blinded scientists to that which has been (seemingly) objectively proven! A famous example is Sir Fred Hoyle who rejected Hawking's presentation of the Big Bang theory despite overwhelming evidence (cosmic microwave background) until his death. Also, scientific bodies who have developed such rigorous testing methods can often build an illusion of objectivity. They sometimes think they are always right just because they came up with the objective method. This results in peer pressure which is borne out of a hierarchical structure which not only led to Darwin publishing his paper on natural selection years after writing it, but also his disgrace.

➤ Ensuring we use rigorous scientific method is the first step (no confounding variables, etc.) to guarding against this mistake. Scientists must also not fully accept a hypothesis just because it appears the logical solution at the time, without any further evidence. Experimentation must be valid and reliable, and peer review is an excellent way of testing these factors. Scientists must welcome other scientists with different prejudices and preferences to follow what they have done to see if the same results are obtained. If they are different, it may well be because of the bias of the first scientists – in this case the scientific method is flawed.

It is an obscenity that rich people can buy better medical treatment than poor people.

➤ The statement argues that it is unfair that wealthier members of society can buy better healthcare than the less well off, suggesting that economic status should not determine one's health. The case is that healthcare is a human right and should thus be available with the same quality to all. In a country where the NHS is widely regarded as the 'crown jewel of the welfare state', it seems contradictory to still have a two tier healthcare system where some can still pay for better healthcare.

➤ One assumption is that private healthcare provides better treatment than public healthcare. Indeed, waiting times are often shorter, but most doctors in private clinics also work with the NHS, and all doctors are trained from the same pool of medical schools. They also use the same scientific knowledge and it is unlikely that a treatment would only be available privately.

➤ Another assumption is that only the rich use private healthcare, but health insurance is now widely available with the rise of relatively cheap insurance companies like BUPA and is included with many jobs.

➤ The NHS (arguably) already provides a good standard of care for all, so if the rich want to spend their disposable income on private healthcare they should be allowed to do so. Not allowing them to spend their money how they wish is breach of their personal rights.

➤ It can be argued that the presence of both systems is actually beneficial to all. The NHS would not be able to cope with the demands of patients using services from both sectors, and waiting times would be increased even further. Those who receive private care still pay taxes to fund the NHS, and they then free up resources for those who are dependent upon it.

➤ The statement can be accepted on an ethical and moral basis, but is not entirely true due to the assumptions it makes, and if we analyse it more thoroughly it appears that the existence of both systems is absolutely necessary.

END OF PAPER

2010

Section 1

Question 1: A

Jay is 150cm tall and has a BMI of 22, so his weight is 49kg. Charlie is 156cm tall and has a BMI of 24, so his weight is 58kg. The combined weight is 172kg, so Alex's BMI must be $172 - 58 - 49 = 65$kg. With a height of 162cm, his BMI is 25.

Question 2: C

This error of reasoning is in the form: x tends to have y, so to increase x we must increase y. However, y may have caused x in the first place. That is, the society being more economically robust may have made the arts flourish in the society, as answer C says.

A is irrelevant to the argument, B may be true, but wouldn't represent a flaw in the argument and D differentiates between the arts, which the argument does not.

Question 3: C

The pupil with the white diamond got the 5th highest on test 1 and the 5th highest on test 2. If you order each set of numbers you will see that the white diamond is Erin.

Question 4: C

The passage talks about the **link** between global warming and spam, and the conclusion must cover both these factors, which none of the other answers do. A is far too general to be a conclusion of the passage which has specific themes. B cannot be inferred because there is no comparison between reducing spam and easing congestion. D is tempting but does not relate to global warming which is the main theme of the passage, and long term effects are not mentioned at all in the passage so is not correct.

Question 5: D

There are 6 batches (72/12). The first batch takes 40 + 25 + 5 minutes (70 minutes), so if they start at 1pm, then the first batch will be done by 2:10. The second batch can be started at 1:40, when the first batch is put into the oven. But after 25 minutes of preparing this second batch, the first batch must be taken out the oven and cooled which takes 5 minutes. So 15 more minutes are required to prepare after this, making preparation 25 + 5 + 15 (45 minutes), and the next batch can be put in at 2:25. Each batch except the first will take 45 minutes to prepare due to this reason, and the oven will never be occupied when it is required so we only need to take this into account until the end.

40 minutes for the first batch + 45 minutes x 5 (for every other batch) = 265 minutes, but we must also include the 30 minutes to cook and cool the final batch, which is 30 minutes. This is 295 minutes in total, which is 5 minutes short of 5 hours, so it takes 4 hours and 55 minutes which amounts to D.

Question 6: B

1 is irrelevant as the argument is that if we did manage to stop burning fossil fuels there would be little effect. If anything, this would further that statement that 'we cannot avoid the disastrous consequences of climate change.' 2 is a fair critique of the argument, as the model they use "assumed that by then CO_2 concentrations would be double preindustrial levels" and this may not be the case if we were able to reduce carbon dioxide significantly. 3 is also irrelevant; other predictions are irrelevant to this argument.

Question 7: B

We know the first digit must be wrong (due to the score limit), and the others are not. If we inspect the similarity of the 8 to other numbers, 3 lights being permanently on could have mean the number was meant to be 2, 5, 6, 9 or 0. The number cannot be 5, 6 or 9 due to the score limit, but can be 0 or 2, so the answer is B.

Question 8: A

The first paragraph suggests that boys and girls preferring to play with different types of toys may have a biological origin rather than a social origin, which means statement A is challenged. B and C are correct according to the first paragraph, meaning they are not 'challenged'. D is irrelevant to the argument in the first paragraph.

Question 9: A

Would be a strong challenge to the study. Whether males or females were dominant, the more aggressive sex taking all the 'attractive' toys, leaving the remaining less 'attractive' toys for the other sex, would mean there is not necessarily a gender preference. B is irrelevant, as there is no talk about how long they keep their interest for. C would actually strengthen the argument, further suggesting that there was a genetic difference causing different preferences. D isn't necessarily a strong challenge, as monkey studies have more bearing on human behaviour than any other species, due to the very similar genetics. E may be true but is irrelevant to the particular topic about preferences based on sex.

Question 10: A

Is clearly an assumption made in the second paragraph, as the study talks about the interest that monkeys have for the objects, and this is measured by the amount of time spent with it. The rest do not necessarily have to be assumed for the claim to be accepted.

Question 11: D

Neither can be inferred from the photographic evidence alone. Showing the male monkey play with a car and the female play with a doll in pictures alone doesn't suggest that the respond in the same way to humans, nor have similar preferences to us. For example, for all we know the car could have been given to the male and the doll given to the female just for the purpose of the photo.

~ 167 ~

Question 12: C

Remove each tile one by one, and see what remains. As we want the proportion of squares of each colour to be equal, and there are 36 squares and 3 colours, we want 36/3 = 12 of each colour, and we only need to test 1 colour to start with.

Removing A leaves 13 blacks, removing B leaves 14 blacks, removing C leaves 12 blacks, removing D leaves 11 blacks and removing E leaves 10 blacks so C must be the correct answer.

Question 13: E

The conclusion of the argument is "Since there will be negative stories in the press either way, we should ignore these stories and not worry about them." This suggests negative stories should be ignored, which is the flaw of the argument. None of the other statements necessarily represent a flaw in the argument.

Question 14: D

This is quite a hard question as there is not really a definite technique to use without wasting too much time. It is the kind of question to come back to at the end and go through systematically at the end if you do happen to have a few minutes spare. You may be able to just spot the most 'different' numbers, however, which is likely to represent the maximum number of elements changing between numbers. Changing between 1 and 6 require 6 changes, and this is the maximum.

Question 15: D

The male child cyclists killed in 2006 was >400 and the female child cyclists killed was <100. This means there were >1700 male pedestrians or cyclists killed and <800 female pedestrians or cyclists, meaning that D is correct.

A is not necessarily true – for example it may be the case that males take more risks, leading to higher risk of death.

B, C and E are not necessarily true – for example, each may be negated by the fact that there may be many more males who ride bikes.

Question 16: D

Visualisation. A cannot be correct – for example if we look at the 6, if the dots were facing this particular direction with 2 rotations it would mean that the 5 should be on top or not in the picture.

B cannot be correct as the 3 can only be in the same position and orientation if it is rotated twice in the SAME direction.

C cannot be correct – for example if we look at the 6 and its orientation, it would mean the 5 should be on the right of it or not in the picture.

E cannot be correct, as at least 1 of the numbers in original picture would remain with 2 different rotations.

Question 17: C

The argument is that safety is ensured by keeping artefacts at the British Museum, citing the example of the Iraqi museum being looted as the evidence that museums in other countries are less safe. However, an example of 1 country doesn't hold for the safety in other countries, so C is the correct answer. The other answers do not represent a flaw in the argument.

Question 18: D

You should use drawings to assist you with this question. 2 ends of the H (2cm each) can fit in the centre of the middle of another H (4cm each), so you can have 6 rows of 3, 2, 3, 2, 3, 2 where they all fit in each other in this way. This allows 15 Hs in 33cm by 24cm.

Question 19: 217

There were 228m passengers at UK airports, and 9 in 10 passengers were travelling internationally, so 10% were travelling on domestic flights. This accounts for 22.8m passengers, and if this was halved to remove the passengers counted twice we would have to take away 11.4m passengers. 228 – 11.4m = 216.6m = 217m passengers.

Question 20: C

There were 34m passenger movements to Spain out of a total of 228m, and 34m/228m represents roughly 15% (10% of 228 is 22.8 and 5% is 11.4). There were roughly 60m passengers in total in 1980 and 15% of this is ~9m.

Question 21: F

All of the answers are correct. 1 is right; the increase between 1955 to 1980 is about 55m and 1980 to 2005 is around 173m, which represents an increase of over treble (still applies if you divide each value by 25 to have the average per annum). Heathrow + Gatwick had 101m passengers, which is greater than 228 x 0.4 (as 10% is 22.8 so 40% must be below 100). In order to reach 500m from 228m, an increase of 272m in 20 years, there must be an average increase in passengers of over 10m a year, as 272/20 > 10.

Question 22: D

The data has been correctly interpreted, using previous results to form a prediction, and this is relevant to the conclusion, so D is correct.

Question 23: E

To work out the permutations, we know that 1 can be matched with any other number except itself, 2 can be matched with any other number except itself and 1 (as this has already been counted), etc. so we have 14 + 13 + 12 + ... + 2 + 1 possibilities which amounts to 105.

We can list the combinations that follow the criteria:

➤   2 with 10, 13, 14 or 15
➤   3 with 10, 12, 14 or 15
➤   4 with 10, 12, 13 or 15
➤   5 with 10, 12, 13 or 14
➤   6 with 10, 12, 13, 14 or 15
➤   7 with 10, 12, 13, 14 or 15
➤   8 and 9 as above

So there are 4 x 4 + 4 x 5 possibilities of this happening, which is 36/105, cancelling to 12/35.

Question 24: C

The argument considers 2 alternatives and suggests one in an implausible explanation, thus concludes the other explanation must be correct. However, other explanations are not considered, so the assumption is that there are no other explanations.
The other statements do not have to be assumed for the argument to hold

Question 25: A

The highest position possible is coming first (alone, not joint first). The other hands add up to 22 (11 doubled for having the same suit), 13 and 11. To beat 22, they can exchange their 2 of spades for their 7 of diamonds from the person who is first, giving them 14, which will be the highest hand (compared to player 1 who now has 6). If the 7 is not taken from player 1 then it is not possible to beat 22.

Question 26: A

The main conclusion of the argument is the first sentence, which is essential paraphrased in A. The other statements can possibly be inferred from the argument but do not address the main conclusion.

Question 27: C

If Phil aims for 4, then there is the possibility of getting 1 and then no guarantee of scoring at least 30.

If he aims for 7, there is the chance of getting 3 and then no guarantee of scoring at least 30.

If he aims for 10, there is the chance of getting 8 and this would mean all 4 darts have not landed in different sections.

If he aims for 11, there is the chance of getting 2, and then no guarantee of scoring at least 30.

If he aims for 9, then he can get 4, 9 or 6. If he gets 4, then he can aim for 6 next time and guarantee over 30. If he gets 9 or 6 he can aim for 5 the next time and guarantee over 30. So C is correct.

Question 28: A

The argument here is that ONLY the name influenced the public opinion i.e. there weren't any other factors swaying public opinion. If statements 2 or 3 were true- the editors and newspaper would have influenced the public with the wording; if 1 was true, the newspaper would have actually reduced bias and the only variable would have been the name used to refer to the child.

Question 29: C

A good way to approach this is to work out the difference of each apple to 200g (what the average of the apples should roughly be), so we have -27, -18, -12, -3, +7, +19 and +24. When we combine three apples we want a total of -3 to +3. This is possible to with -27, +19 and +7 which adds up to -1, and -18, -3 and +24 which adds up to +3. This leaves us with -12 which is 188g.

~ 172 ~

Question 30: B

It is not assumed that expensive schemes are not justified, the argument instead states that the particular idea of reducing class sizes is not justified for other reasons (and the fact that is expensive is just an additional point instead of a reason for not supporting it).

A is assumed in "candidates with lower qualifications would have to be recruited."

C is assumed in "California had risen only to 48th…"

D is assumed in the final sentence.

Question 31: D

Spatial reasoning questions in the BMAT are always hard. The key here was to analyse the relationship of the shapes e.g. the white square must be the opposite face to the cross. Then you need to look for nets that don't satisfy these relationships e.g. Net B would put the white square and cross next to each other rather than opposite. Keep finding more relationships to exclude the options. If you're really stuck, take scissors into your exam (get it approved by your exam centre before though!).

Question 32: C

The average annual income for the bottom 20% is roughly between 16,200 and 17,300, which is 16,750. For the top 20% it is roughly between 50,000 and 160,000, which is 105,000. 6:1 appears to be the closest ratio to 105:16.75, and this can be roughly checked by seeing that 17 x 6 is 102.

Question 33: C

We can work this out by dividing the top 10%'s average income (~160k) by all the other values added together. Rounding is fine (and advised), so we have 16k + 17k + 19k + 20k + 22k + 26k + 30k + 37k + 51k + 160k which is 400k. 160/400 = 2/5 = 40%

Question 34: C

20% of the top 10% is about 160k x 0.2 = 32k, and 20% of the next top 10% is roughly 50k x 0.2 = 10k, giving 42k to distribute. If this was spread out between the other 80%, each 10% block would receive 42k/8 each, which is 5.25k. $16,200 + $5,250 is close to $21,500.

Question 35 B

1 is incorrect as the data does not concern people within a given country, only between different countries. 2 is correct as the left graph shows that countries with a lower level of inequality and hence variability have generally healthier people.

END OF SECTION

Section 2

Question 1: E

The hypothalamus detects changes in temperature. Arterioles dilate so that more heat can radiate out the body, keeping the body cool. Knowing these two factors alone will get you the correct answer.

For completeness, the hair erector muscles contract and capillaries in the skin do not move.

Question 2: E

$$Moles\ of\ Iodine\ = \frac{63.5}{127} = 0.5\ moles$$

$$Moles\ of\ Oxygen\ = \frac{20}{16} = 1.25\ moles$$

Thus the molar ratio is 2 moles of iodine to 5 moles of oxygen. I.e. I_2O_5

Question 3: A

After the end of experiment (12 minutes) there is 16g of U-234. Thus, there must have been 16g of Protactinium-234 at the start. The time at which the mass of Protactinium-234 is half its initial value (8g) is 1.2 minutes.

Question 4: C

The big container is full to start with, representing 1 unit of water. If they contain the same amount of water after pouring, each will have 0.5 units of water. The larger container thus contains 0.5 units out of a total of 1.

$$P\ = \frac{0.5}{Capacity} = \frac{0.5}{1} = 0.5.$$

The smaller container contains 0.5 units of water but out of a total possible volume of **less than 1** as it is a smaller container. Since Q = 0.5/Capacity, and the capacity is less than 1, Q must be > 0.5 (because dividing 0.5 by a number <1 results in a number >0.5

$\sim 175 \sim$

Question 5: C

Insulin reduces blood glucose levels by promoting the uptake of glucose into cells. Statements 2 and 3 are correct.

Question 6: D

12g of carbon = 1 mole of carbon. In the first equation, 1 mole of carbon is used. In the second equation, the initial one mole from equation 1 and an additional mole is used to produce 2CO. Thus, 2 moles of carbon are used. In the final equation, 3CO produces $3CO_2$. However, since only 2 moles of CO were produced in equation 2, only 2 moles of CO_2 are produced.

Thus, the mass of 2 moles of $CO_2 = 2 \, x \, [12 + (2 \, x \, 16)] = 88g$

Question 7: A

$$Amplitude = \frac{peak - trough}{2} = \frac{6}{2} = 3$$

$$Frequency = \frac{1}{period} = \frac{1}{12 \, x \, 60 \, x \, 60}$$

$$Frequency = \frac{1}{12 \, x \, 3600}$$

Question 8: C

This is easier than it appears. To get back to where they started, the player must go in the opposite direction to whence they came, and the same distance. The player has a ¼ chance to go the opposite direction, and a ¼ chance to go the same distance which gives: $\frac{1}{4} x \frac{1}{4} = \frac{1}{16}$

Question 9: B

Geographic distribution is irrelevant for an individual, and a high reproductive capacity is an effect rather than a cause of natural selection. A gene pool refers to all of the alleles in a person or population. Natural selection will favour an advantageous allele within this gene pool.

Question 10: D

This is one you just have to know! The complete combustion of a fuel produces water and carbon dioxide. If you were unsure, then think about the combustion of clean hydrocarbon fuels like propane etc which result in the production of H_2O and CO_2.

Question 11: C

An alpha particle contains 2 protons and 2 neutrons. Thus, the emission of 3 alpha particles will reduce the mass number by 12 and the atomic number by 6.

In beta decay, a neutron decays into a proton and electron. Thus, two rounds of beta decay will result increase the atomic number by 2.

Overall, the atomic number decreases by 4 from 86 → 82 and the atomic mass decreases by 12 from 219 → 207.

Question 12: C

$$Mean = \frac{total\ time\ for\ all\ people}{Number\ of\ people} = 56$$

First group total time $= 20 \ x \ 54 = 1080$

Second group total time $= T \ x \ P$

Substitute into original equation:

$$Mean = \frac{1080 + PT}{20 + P} = 56$$

This simplifies to: $PT - 56P = 1120 - 1080$

$P(T - 56) = 40$

$$P = \frac{40}{T - 56}$$

~ 177 ~

Question 13: F

1. Incorrect - transmitter molecules are recognised by their receptors, but are not formed in them.
2. Incorrect - the signal is transmitted by diffusion, as osmosis only applies to water.
3. Incorrect - transmitter molecules CAUSE the signal to be transmitted across the synapse.

Statements 4 and 5 are correct.

Question 14: A

The key here is that ionic equations must be balanced for charge **and** stoichiometry. Only equations 1, 2 and 6 balance for both of these.

➤ For Equation 3: Adding 2 electrons to O^{2-} forms O^{4-}
➤ Equation 4: Taking an electron away from O^{2-} forms O^{-}
➤ For Equation 5: Taking 2 electrons away from $2I^{-}$ produces $2I$.

Question 15: B

Before the changes were made, all of the charge would bypass the 4 parallel bulbs through switch Q, so bulb Y will have the entire 12V running through it. Afterwards, all bulbs will have some charge flowing through them, so bulb X will be brighter than before and bulb Y will be dimmer than before.

Question 16: C

Notice that triangles ABC and ADE are similar. Thus: $\frac{BC}{BA} = \frac{DE}{DA}$

This gives: $\frac{x}{4} = \frac{x+3}{x}$

Cross-multiply to give: $x^2 = 4x + 12$

This sets up the quadratic equation: $x^2 - 4x - 12 = 0$

$(x - 6)(x + 2) = 0$

Since length must be a positive value, $x = 6$. Thus, $DE = x + 3$

$= 6 + 3 = 9\,cm$

Question 17: E

S, T and U do not have the condition, but could be carriers as their parents both carried the recessive allele. U must be a carrier as X has the condition and this is not possible if one parent does not have a recessive allele.

Since P and Q are carriers, the probability of both S and T being carriers is 50%.

Question 18: B

This question requires balancing the charges to equal 0:

A.   A gives a charge of -2
B.   B gives a charge of 0. H_2PO_4 has a charge of -1, so 2 of these groups balance the +2 on the Mg^{2+} ion.
C.   C gives a charge of +2
D.   D gives a charge of +2
E.   E gives a charge of +2
F.   F gives a charge of +3.

Question 19: B

Acceleration can be determined from velocity-time graphs but not distance-time graphs so we can immediately rule out R and S.

➤ $Acceleration = \frac{\Delta velocity}{\Delta time} = \frac{\Delta y}{\Delta x}$

➤ In P, $Acceleration = \frac{10}{24} = 0.42 \ ms^{-2}$

➤ In Q, $Acceleration = \frac{48}{20} = 2.4 \ ms^{-2}$

Question 20: A

$Total\ SA\ =\ area\ of\ 2\ circular\ sections\ +\ longitudinal\ area$

$=\ 2\pi r^2 + 2\pi rh$

$Volume\ = \pi r^2 h$

Since Volume = Surface area: $2\pi r^2 + 2\pi rh = \pi r^2 h$

Simply to give: $2r + 2h = rh$

$2r = rh - 2h$

$h = \frac{2r}{r-2}$

Question 21: B

Statements 3 and 4 are the wrong way around; meiosis results in four nuclei and mitosis results in two nuclei. All the other statements are correct.

Question 22: C

$A_r\ of\ benzene\ =\ (6\ x\ 12)\ +\ (6\ x\ 1) = 78$

$Moles\ of\ benzene\ = \frac{3.9}{78}\ =\ 0.05\ moles$

$A_r\ of\ nitrobenzene\ =\ (6\ x\ 12) + 5\ + 14 + (2\ x\ 16) = 123$

$Moles\ of\ nitrobenzene\ = \frac{3.69}{123} =\ 0.03\ moles$

$\%\ Yield\ = \frac{0.03}{0.05} =\ 60\%$

Question 23: G

$$Power \ = \ \frac{work\ done}{time} \ = \ \frac{Force\ x\ Distance}{time}$$

The force is the weight of the water $= \ mg \ = \ 5\ x\ 10 \ = \ 50N$

Thus, $Power \ = \ \frac{50\ x\ 5}{1} = 250\ W$

Using $v^2 \ = \ u^2 \ + \ 2as$:

$0 \ = \ u^2 \ + \ (2)x(-10)x(5)$

$u^2 = 100$

$u = 10\ ms^{-1}$

Question 24: C

This is a time consuming question and one you should consider leaving till the end as it could easily consume several minutes of your precious time.

Let the biggest square have a side length of 1 unit.

Second Square:

The sides of the second square are $\frac{1}{3}\ x\ 1$ and $\frac{2}{3}\ x\ 1$.

Using Pythagoras's theorem:

$$c^2 \ = \ \left(\frac{1}{3}\right)^2 \ + \ \left(\frac{2}{3}\right)^2 = \frac{1}{9} + \frac{4}{9}$$

$$c \ = \ \sqrt{\frac{5}{9}} = \frac{\sqrt{5}}{3}$$

Third Square:

The sides of the third square are $\frac{2}{3} x \frac{\sqrt{5}}{3}$ and $\frac{1}{3} x \frac{\sqrt{5}}{3}$

$$= \frac{2\sqrt{5}}{9} \text{ and } \frac{\sqrt{5}}{9}$$

Using Pythagoras's theorem:

$$c^2 = \left(\frac{2\sqrt{5}}{9}\right)^2 + \left(\frac{\sqrt{5}}{9}\right)^2 = \frac{4x5}{81} + \frac{5}{81}$$

$$c = \sqrt{\frac{25}{81}} = \frac{5}{9}$$

Fourth Square:

The sides of the fourth square are $\frac{2}{3} x \frac{5}{9}$ and $\frac{1}{3} x \frac{5}{9}$

$$= \frac{10}{27} \text{ and } \frac{5}{27}$$

Using Pythagoras's theorem:

$$c^2 = \left(\frac{10}{27}\right)^2 + \left(\frac{5}{27}\right)^2 = \frac{100}{27^2} + \frac{25}{27^2}$$

$$c = \sqrt{\frac{125}{27^2}}$$

The area of the fourth square $= \sqrt{\frac{125}{27^2}} \ x \ \sqrt{\frac{125}{27^2}} = \frac{125}{729}$

Question 25: E

Statements 1 and 4 ignore the fact that the nervous system also uses chemical transmission at the synapse. The other statements are correct.

Question 26: B

Don't be perturbed- this is a free mark. Count all the corners of the structure (don't double count if they overlap) (= 17) and the carbons on the functional groups (=3) to give a total of 20 carbon atoms.

Question 27: D

The engine is doing work against the gravity **AND** against the frictional force. Since the car moves 50m along the road, it has gained $\frac{50}{20} = 2.5m$ in height. Thus:

$$Total\ work\ is\ =\ Work\ vs.\ gravity\ +\ Work\ vs.\ Frictional\ force$$

$$Work\ vs.\ gravity\ =\ Gain\ in\ Gravitational\ potential\ energy$$
$$E_p\ =\ 800\ x\ 10\ x\ 2.5\ =\ 20,000\ J$$

$$Work\ vs.\ Frictional\ force\ =\ Force\ x\ Distance$$
$$=\ 500\ x\ 50\ =\ 25,000 J$$
$$Total\ Work\ Done\ =\ 20,000\ +\ 25,000$$
$$=\ 45,000\ J\ =\ 45\ kJ$$

END OF SECTION

Section 3

Anyone who has a serious ambition to be a president or prime minister is the wrong kind of person for the job.

➢ 'Serious ambition' is considered a negative in this statement whereby somebody will scheme, conspire and exceed the boundaries of morality with the sole view of personal gain. It is previously been revealed that many world leaders have been willing to sacrifice their values, loyalty and even family in order to maximise their power at all costs.

➢ The head of a state or government is intended to be a role model and representative of the people. However, those that have dedicated their entire lives to pursue their aspiration of leading a country are more likely to lie, pander, compromise their principles, steal votes, be corrupt, manipulate the press and manipulate public opinion; traits that most of 'the people' would frown upon and consider morally unacceptable. These attributes, especially corruption, may also have longer lasting effects and lead to stunted societal and economic progress.

➢ If those that lead have the trait of over-ambition, it is also likely that they have idealistic and possibly even extreme views which are likely to conflict with those of the people. And, in a democracy, it is meant that the majority has a say, which is clearly compromised in this situation.

➢ However, some level of motivation and drive is necessary to lead a country. An ambitious attitude can lead anyone to triumph and satisfaction, which is extremely desirable for somebody that a country is meant to look up to. They will strive to perform the best they can in their role and they love the determined, passionate person they are determined to become and the feeling their work gives them, so they find no reason to quit and always aim for the very best outcomes.

➢ Ultimately need a balance of ambition without crossing any legal or moral boundaries.

People injured whilst participating in extreme sports should not be treated by a publicly funded health service.

➤ The statement argues that those participating in extreme sports knowledgeably put their health at risk and treating them on a publicly funded health service is unfair and ultimately a burden to society. The NHS has limited resources, and those who partake in these sports are more likely to require this time and money, which is borne from the taxpayers' pockets even if they themselves did not undertake such risky behaviour. This may result in reduced resources available to treat other illnesses which were not self-inflicted.

➤ In public healthcare, there should be the unstated duty to keep oneself healthy; treating patients who are not keeping themselves healthy removes the responsibility for one's own health. Indeed, in a private- or insurance-based healthcare arrangement those who encounter more hazards would be expected to pay a higher premium.

➤ However, all taxpayers pay money to the government to fund the health service, and have a right to use the facilities they have paid for. Their autonomy as contributors must be respected; we should avoid judgement and allow them to live their life as they please. It would be unfair to single participants of extreme sports as the only group not to receive treatment. The Hippocratic Oath pledges that doctors should treat all patients without exception.

➤ Everything in life is risky to some extent. One could argue, with the same logic, that drivers know the risk of having a car crash so we should not treat them if an accident were to occur.

➤ Moreover, many other illnesses and diseases that are similarly 'self-inflicted', such as those caused by smoking, excessive drinking, unsafe sex, overeating, etc. are treatable on the NHS. If we were to deny funding for those doing extreme sports, this would generate a slippery slope where other diseases were debated for exclusion from public healthcare.

> ➢ Impossible to draw a line between an accident and self-inflicted disease, and thus whether somebody would qualify for treatment depending on the risk of the action which caused the injury.

> ➢ Allowing patient autonomy key in the healthcare system, as is showing beneficence.

A pet belongs to its owner - it is their property. Thus, if a client asks for their healthy cat to be painlessly euthanized, a veterinary clinician should always agree to this request.

> ➢ The statement suggests that as a pet is the direct property of the owner, their wishes relating to decisions regarding the pet should be complied with, regardless of its condition.
> ➢ There is some support for this argument; there are many cases whereby an owner neglected a pet after euthanasia has been refused, causing more pain and suffering than a painless death at a surgery. It is true that vets are not obliged to perform euthanasia on healthy animals but if an owner is determined that euthanasia is the only option, the stress for the animal of being taken to numerous other clinics when the outcome is inevitable can be argued as unethical.
> ➢ However, if an owner is determined to let go of their pet, there are many options that avoid unnecessary murder. Relocation to a new, caring home or adoption to an animal shelters are both schemes that are heavily supported in this country. The definition of euthanasia is to prevent prolonged suffering and if the pet is healthy there is no need to kill it prematurely.
> ➢ Animals have rights and one of those is the right to live. In a similar fashion to the argument, children under 18 are considered by law the 'property' of their parents, but it would be thought ludicrous if a healthy child was pushed to be euthanised by their parents.
> ➢ Undoubtedly the owners are extremely important in the lives of pets, and should have influence in decisions relating to them. This does not mean necessarily mean, however, that the owners have the right to harm their pet.

Science only tells us what is possible, not what is right.

➤ Science has made astonishing progress in the pursuit answering the questions about how the universe works, and is based on empirical evidence rather than beliefs. It allows us to call a friend living on the other side of the world, has answered how the hole in the ozone layer formed and helps us determine how best to treat a patient suffering from diabetes.

➤ Science finds truth based on rational reasoning allowing objectivity, whereas opinions and natural biases would lead to subjectivity. Sam Harris, a famous neuroscientist, argues that most ethical question arise due to neurobiological factors and to answer them a thorough understanding of the brain is required.

➤ However, it is worth noting that even things we usually consider to be scientific fact, are actually termed 'theories', e.g. Germ Theory, the Theory of Relativity and even the Theory of Evolution. The nature of scientific theory means it is always open to falsification.

➤ Science helps us describe how the world is, and what we are able to do and achieve, but it doesn't help us make moral judgements about whether that state of affairs is right or wrong. Examples include animal rights and euthanasia.

➤ Science can't help us make aesthetic or artistic judgements - e.g. whether a painting or a piece of music is good or bad.

➤ Science doesn't necessarily tell you how to use the scientific knowledge. For example, when new knowledge about recombinant DNA may become available, but this doesn't mean one knows whether to use this knowledge to correct a genetic disease, develop a bruise-resistant apple, or construct a new bacterium. For almost any important scientific advance, one can imagine both positive and negative ways that knowledge could be used. Other examples: Hiroshima atom bomb, designer babies, most 'painless' way to kill an animal.

➤ If it weren't for science's exploration for rational, objective answers, we wouldn't begin to consider the moral issues concerning what is right and wrong; science doesn't tell us what is right but it is necessary more indirectly.

END OF PAPER

2011

Section 1

Question 1: D

Assign each row to a bar chart based on relative values and values that are the same. Max temperature is E, wind speed is C, rain is B and cloud cover is A. D remains.

Question 2: E

None of the answers are conclusions that can be drawn from the passage. A implies a causation between the noise of modern human life and extinction which is not a conclusion of the passage. The passage doesn't suggest sea-based wind farms shouldn't be built so B is wrong. 'Should not' is a very bold statement and is usually involved in an incorrect answer.

Although the passage mentions that the whales are trying to adapt their communication methods, 'will be able to adapt' is too strong a phrase and thus C is wrong.

D is tempting but there is nothing to suggest that the depletion was initially caused by the growth of human noise.

Question 3: C

There is lots of irrelevant information in this question, but the maths is quite easy. Deluxe rooms are $80 a night, but there is $15 less per night being paid for no meals, so that is $65 x 6 for the room. Hiring a car is $5 + $5 x 6 (there is no taxi use). $65 x 6 + $5 + $5 x 6 = $425.

Question 4: E

The argument assumes that children either interact with each other OR play computer games, so E is correct. The other answers may be 'correct' from your previous knowledge but are unrelated to the argument. The argument is about the link between children playing computer games and social interaction, which the other answers do not address.

Question 5: F

This can be visualised to rule out 1 and 2. Also, 1 is the same as the right hand mirror, and 2 is a rotated version of the left hand mirror, which means they cannot be reflected images.

Question 6: C

The conclusion of the passage is "so all that learning...increases their memory power." This suggests that the fact their brain areas related to memory are more developed is through being a taxi driver rather than their predispositions. The other answers are not assumptions that are made in the argument.

Question 7: A

You can start by ruling out C, E and F as the range of miles per journey is too low. Out of the rest, you must work out the best fuel consumption per passenger mile. You can do this by finding out the lowest value of: fuel consumption of empty plane + fuel consumption per passenger x number of passengers. If we use 177 passengers and the values for each plane, it is easy to see that A will be the lowest per mile.

Question 8: D

Women in their 40s or 50s earned over 20% less than men on average, meaning they earned less than £0.80 for every £1 earned by a man in that range. A cannot be reliably concluded as we only have information about relative pay rather than absolute pay. B cannot be concluded, as we don't have definite information about how willing employers are to employ women based on age. C cannot be concluded, as we don't know the difference between the pay gap at the ages of 22 and 30; we only have information for the whole ranges (22-29 and 30-39).

Question 9: D – should be C?

If we call male pay m, we see from the equation given that $22.8 = 100 \times (m-16000)/m$
If we rearrange the equation we find that $m = 16000/0.772$. We need to be careful about rounding as there is a low range between the answers, but if we begin to do short division of $1600000/77$ we can see that 207xx are the first 3 digits, making C the best estimate.

Question 10: C

The assumption is that the long hours and intensity of senior positions deterred mothers in particular, but they would be happy to take these positions in any other case, which is said in C. The other answers are irrelevant.

Question 11: D

Is the only answer that could be correct, and satisfies the maths too: using estimates we know $(15-9)/15 \times 100 = 40\%$. There is no information about part-time workers over 60 so A cannot be correct. B and C assume that absolute wage values are known, whereas we only have relative proportions.

Question 12: D

There are 6 types: fully white, fully black, ¼ outlined, ¼ outlined, ¼ black, ¼ black with the other quarters outlined.

Question 13: B

Would definitely strengthen the HAR1 hypothesis. A lack of native HAR1 causes language impairment, suggesting that it is necessary for human language ability.

A, if anything, would weaken the hypothesis as the hypothesis suggests that it is the uniqueness of HAR1 that allows human language ability.

C, D and E don't strengthen the hypothesis as they are irrelevant to human language ability.

Question 14: C

Each team played 4 matches, and we can determine how many wins, draws and losses each team had. With 2 points, Central must have drawn 2 and lost 2. With 8, Northern must have won 2 and drawn 2. Southern must have won 1, drawn 2 and lost 1 whilst Western must have drawn 1 and lost 3. The discrepancies (3 wins and 6 losses) mean that Eastern must have won 3 and drawn 1.

Question 15: B

1 is incorrect as the argument is not about who, in particular, defines the human rights, and 3 is irrelevant to the argument. 2 is correct because the passage assumes something cannot be both a constitutional right and human right; it can only be one or the other.

Question 16: D

Area is length x width, and volume is area x depth. So all we need here volume/width to determine the highest value for depth. Don't waste time working out answers for lakes that are not an answer, and we don't need to use exact numbers. For example, Caspian Sea's depth is 78,200/394,299 which we can think of as 80,000/400,000 which is roughly 0.2 km. When we do the same for the others, Baikal clearly has the highest depth which is around 0.67 km

Question 17: C

1 isn't an assumption made: the argument doesn't require the assumption that most of the population have eaten beef infected with BSE. In fact, the main conclusion is that there will be further outbreaks in the future as those who consumed the infected beef grow older, and this is irrelevant to how many have eaten the beef. 2 is clearly incorrect, as the argument discusses that inheriting the V variant in the M-V combination can lead to developing vCJD in later life. 3 is correct as the argument assumes the combination of genes is the most important factor rather than the M variant itself.

Question 18: B

Jasper earns £240 + £5 x 22 + £20 x 6 = £470 per week, so Ruby earns £510 per week. Ruby is 35, and if we call her years worked as y, £240 + £5 x 14 + £20 x y = £510, and y = 10. This means Ruby has worked for 4 more years than Jasper.

Question 19: A

The sum of the possible outcomes for drilling is -720000 x 0.1 + 400000 x 0.8 + 3800000 x 0.1 = $628000
The sum of possible outcomes for not drilling is 1000000 x 0.2 + 500000 x 0.6 = 500000.
So drilling represents a more favourable option than not drilling.

Question 20: D

Is correct – the probability of a 'medium' strike is 0.8, as is the probability of selling the drilling rights at $500,000 or $1,000,000 (0.6 + 0.2). A is incorrect, as a medium strike allows a profit too. B is incorrect, as $400,000 x 0.8 is less than $500,000. C is incorrect, as there is only a 0.1 chance of making a loss, and a 0.9 chance (medium or big strike) of making a profit.

Question 21: F

All of the answers are correct. The costs would be £1,300,000 for drilling, which is higher than the returns for a medium strike (£1,200,000). The only way to make a profit is thus a big strike, which has a 10% chance. They could however make a profit if they reduced drilling costs by 25% to £600,000, so costs would be £1,100,000, which is lower than the returns for a medium strike.

Question 22: E

The sum of expected outcomes for drilling is $628,000 and is $500,000 for not drilling. Paying the insurance would make the value for drilling $428,000. Without insurance, the expected outcome for an oil spill is -$10,000,000 x 0.03 = $300,000, making the value for drilling $328,000. Not drilling has a value of $500,000. So the order is 3, 1, 2.

Question 23: D

Determine which numbers haven't been used. On the left side the remaining numbers must add up to 13, and must be 6 and 7, but we don't know which order. On the right hand side they must add up to 10, so they are 8 and 2 but we don't know which order. This mean the number right of 9 must be 4, and the remaining 2 numbers must add up to 8 on this row, which must be 6 and 2. So between 5 and 3 is 7.

Question 24: A

The quote means Fredericks will not play if Petermass is fit, and may or may not play if Petermass is not fit. This makes 1 correct and 2 and 3 incorrect.

Question 25: C

The one with equal proportions has 90ml of oil and vinegar and the other has 120ml oil and 60ml vinegar. So if we add half of the one with equal proportions to the other, we have 45ml of each in the first and we have 165ml oil and 105ml vinegar in the other. This latter one represents 11/18 oil and 7/18 vinegar. If 90ml of this mix is taken, 55ml will be oil and 35ml will be vinegar. So there will be 110ml oil in one (165-55) and 100ml (45+55) in the other.

Question 26: C

This is the correct answer as the argument talks of the possibility that many planets could support human life.
A is not correct as gravity is not the only factor that determines whether a planet can support life.
B is not necessarily correct and the use of the word 'must' means it is probably too bold a statement.
D is tempting but the passage uses the words 'probably in the order of 10 or 20 per cent', so saying it is 10 or 20 percent is too strong.
E is again too bold a statement, as the passage only says that there 'could be' tens of billions of these systems.

Question 27: A

This is easier than it looks. The question is asking if you can form a 6 x 2 or a 4 x 3 rectangle with 3 of the shapes. However, it's not actually possible to form a rectangle of those dimensions regardless of the shapes you pick.

Question 28: C

2 is not necessary information for the argument; the distance that each bus needs to travel every week is irrelevant, so C must be the correct answer. We can check and see that the other points are reasonable, which they are.

Question 29: D

3km from the library is the distance when Claire leaves 20 minutes late. This tells you that when Claire leaves on time she is 1km from the library when Charles is 3km away (she walks 2km in 20 minutes so had she left on time she would be 2km further along). As they usually meet at the Library, Charles has to cover 3km while she covers 1km, so he cycles 3 times faster than she walks at 18km/hr.

Question 30: B

Paraphrases the last 2 sentences of the passage and is the correct answer. A and D are both too bold to be answers as the passage highlights that it is just a theory. C isn't correct as we don't know if it is the best explanation – we haven't heard any other hypotheses.

Question 31: C

There are 20 cans remaining. The view from X shows us that there are 6 cans in the shaded columns remaining. Thus, there are 14 cans in the 6 columns in the middle. Thus, a maximum of 4 cans can be missing 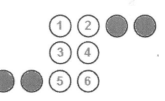 from the middle 6 columns. Options A, B, E and F are too full to not be possible. D is still possible if columns 3 and 4 only have one can each (therefore columns 1-6 = 14). Only C is therefore not possible as columns 1 and 2 would have to be 2 cans tall and columns 3 and 4 to be 1 can tall (6 cans missing).

Question 32: C

Rounding is ok here because of the big difference between answers. 1500 patients per doctor, so a total of 1500 x 5 consultations a year = 7500 consultations a year per doctor. 7500/250 = 30 consultations a day, and C is the closest (it would be closer to 32 if we didn't round down earlier).

Question 33: D

The proportion in 1995 was 0.8/3.29 which is close to 0.2, and was 1.8/5.26 in 2006 which is close to 0.33. The percentage increase is (0.33-0.20)/0.20 x 100 which is roughly 65%, making D the closest.

Question 34: C

C is clearly the only viable answer, as the ratio is definitely above 2 between 15 and 35 and then starts to decrease towards 1.

Question 35: C

People may have become 11 years older, but there is still the same age group within the age demographics, so ageing is irrelevant. The others are relevant.

END OF SECTION

Section 2

Question 1: F

Carbohydrase is an enzyme – not a gland, hormone or a function so does not fit into the table. All the other words/statements fit in somewhere.

Question 2: B

X has 3 electrons in its outer most electron shell and Y needs 2 electrons to make a complete outer electron shell. I.e. Valency of X is +3 and Y is -2. The easy way to figure out formulae is to 'swap' the valencies to give: X_2Y_3.

Question 3: C

Remember that $E_k = \frac{mv^2}{2}$ and $E_p = mg\Delta h$

Since E_k is proportional to velocity^2, doubling the velocity means E_k is 4 times higher. E_p is proportional to height so doubling the height means E_p is 2 times greater. Thus, C is the correct answer.

Question 4: C

$$3x\left(3x^{-\frac{1}{3}}\right)^3$$

$$= 3x\left(3^3 x^{-\frac{3}{3}}\right)$$

$$= 3x(27x^{-1})$$

$$= 3x\left(\frac{27}{x}\right)$$

$$= 81$$

Question 5: F

Mitosis produces genetically identical cells and meiosis results in variation so 1 and 2 are wrong. Statements 3,4 and 5 are correct.

Question 6: D

Raising the temperature increases the average kinetic energy of all molecules. Thus, more collisions take place per unit time and the average collision has more energy. However, temperature has no effect on the orientation of the molecules.

Question 7: E

A. Nuclear fission is the splitting of a nucleus into 2 small parts. Whilst gamma radiation may be released, this is not the definition of fission.
B. The half life of a radioactive substance is the time taken for half of it to decay (not half the time for it to decay).
C. The number of neutrons is given by the mass number – atomic number, not the other way around.
D. Nuclear power stations utilise fission, not fusion.
E. A beta particle consists of a highly charged electron. There is no change in the atomic mass.
F. When a nucleus emits an alpha particle, it loses 2 neutrons + 2 protons.

Question 8: D

At 9:45 the hour hand will be ¾ of the way to 10 from 9 and the minutes hand will be at 9. The number of degrees between the hours is $\frac{360}{12} = 30$. Thus ¾ of this is 22.5 degrees.

Question 9: C

4 is incorrect because individuals with relatively disadvantageous adaptations will still usually be able to breed, unless that adaptation actually causes death or an inability to breed. The other statements are correct.

Question 10: D

Each carbon atom can make 4 bonds and each hydrogen atom can make 1 bond. So the outer carbons are bonded to 2 hydrogens each. However, the carbon atoms between the two rings are only bound to 1 hydrogen. So if we count up, there are 10 carbons and 18 hydrogens.

Thus, $A_r = (12 \times 10) + (1 \times 18) = 138$

Question 11: B

Be careful! The current in this circuit flows clockwise (most circuits are anticlockwise). The diode is thus a break in the circuit in this direction. When the switch is open, we have 2 breaks in the circuit, so no current can flow through either of the branches. Thus, the reading on the ammeter will be 0. When the switch is closed, the current can pass through the branch without the diode in it. Since the resistance is 3 ohms and voltage is 6V:

$$I = \frac{6}{3} = 2 A$$

Question 12: D

The quickest way to solve this is via trial and error- assign values to each option to see if you can disprove them e.g. If W is 3 and x is 2, then option A would be incorrect (yet the inequalities in the question would still hold). The only inequality that **must** be true is x > y because $y^2 < x$.

Question 13: E

Oxygen and carbon dioxide move across membranes via diffusion, not osmosis. Oxygenated blood goes to muscles and deoxygenated blood returns from muscles. The oxygen concentration is low in the muscle cells as oxygen is required for aerobic respiration, and carbon dioxide is high because it is produced during aerobic respiration. Thus:

➢ CO_2 is high in muscles and low in plasma.
➢ O_2 is high in RBC and low in muscle.
➢ Hence, E is correct.

~ 199 ~

Question 14: C

A metal cannot form covalent bonds with a non-metal, so NaCl and Na_2O are ionic compounds. All the other compounds contain a covalent bonds.

Question 15: B

This is a good example of why it's handy to know the suvat equations as it can save you a lot of time.

Using $v^2 = u^2 + 2as$

$0^2 = 300^2 + 2 \, x \, a \, x \, 0.6$

Thus, $0 = 90000 + 1.2a$

$a = \frac{9 \, x \, 10^4}{1.2} = 7.5 \, x \, 10^4$

Now use $F = ma$ to give: $F = 0.05 \, x \, 7.5 \, x \, 10^4$

$F = 0.375 \, x \, 10^4 = 3.75 \, x \, 10^3 N$

Question 16: E
Don't try to solve these algebraically – its much quicker to sketch them!

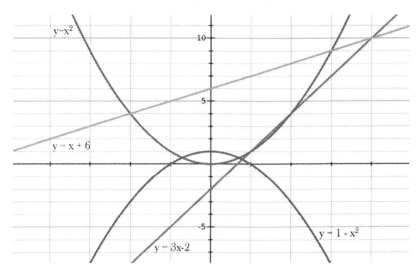

As is easily visible, $y = 1 - x^2$ and $y = x + 6$ don't intersect. Thus, the answer is E.

Question 17: D

Any are feasible. The condition could be dominant with P, Q, R and S having the recessive alleles only. The sperm from T could have carried the allele from the condition, or a mutation could have been present in an egg of S.

Question 18: E

The easiest way to solve this is to set up your own algebraic equation for Oxygen (as it appears the most number of times):

$3B = 6X + Y + 2$

Then simply see if any of the options satisfy this equation- only option E does. If you're unsure about how to setup these equations then check out the chemistry chapter in *The Ultimate BMAT Guide*.

Question 19: A

The current flowing through a resistor at a constant temperature is directly proportional to the potential difference across it. Thus, as voltage increases, current increases at a constant rate i.e. resistance does not change.

Question 20: B

This is a test of how quickly you can use Pythagoras's theorem:

Bottom Triangle:
The hypotenuse is given by $= \sqrt{1^2 + 3^2} = \sqrt{10}$

Middle Triangle:

Since the triangles are similar, the small edge must be 1/3 of $\sqrt{10} = \frac{\sqrt{10}}{3}$

The hypotenuse is given by $= \sqrt{\left(\sqrt{10}\right)^2 + \left(\frac{\sqrt{10}}{3}\right)^2} = \sqrt{10 + \frac{10}{9}}$

$= \sqrt{\frac{90+10}{9}}$

$= \sqrt{\frac{100}{9}} = \frac{10}{3}$

Top Triangle:

Since the triangles are similar, the small edge must be 1/3 of $\frac{10}{3} = \frac{10}{9}$

The area of the triangle $= \frac{1}{2} \, base \; x \; height = \frac{1}{2} x \frac{10}{9} x \frac{10}{3}$

$= \frac{100}{54} = \frac{50}{27} \; cm^2$

Question 21: D

Cell P is haploid and can be any sex cell. Cell Q is diploid and can be almost any somatic cell. Cell R can be enucleated, or a red blood cells (because they have no nucleus). Only D satisfies these criteria.

Question 22: D

The mass of PbS in the ore $= 70\% \; of \; 478kg$

$= \frac{70}{100} \; x \; 478 = 335 \; kg$

The atomic mass of PbS $= 207 + 32 = 239$

The proportion of lead in PbS $= \frac{207}{239} \approx \frac{210}{240} = 0.875$

Thus, the mass of lead that can be extracted $= 0.875 \; x \; 335 = 293 \; kg$

The closest answer to this is 289.8 kg.

NB: Remember rounding numbers to make the maths easier also means you won't get the **exact** answer on the paper. Thus, always check the options to see how much room you have to round numbers. If they are close together then you should avoid rounding and vice versa.

Question 23: C

Light travels slower in glass than air, but its frequency remains the same. Since $c = f\lambda$, wavelength must decrease to accommodate for the lower speed. Option C is the only one that satisfies these requirements.

Question 24: B

12 can only be achieved by rolling 2 sixes.

The probability of rolling a 6 on the fair die = 1/6

$P(12) = P(6 \text{ on fair die}) \times P(6 \text{ on unfair die})$

$\frac{1}{18} = \frac{1}{6} \times P(6 \text{ on unfair die})$

Thus, $P(6 \text{ on unfair die}) = \frac{1}{3}$

$P(1 \text{ to } 5 \text{ on unfair die}) = 1 - \frac{1}{3} = \frac{2}{3}$

$P(1 \text{ on unfair die}) = \frac{\frac{2}{3}}{5} = \frac{2}{15}$

2 can only be achieved by rolling 2 ones.

$P(2) = P(1 \text{ on fair die}) \times P(1 \text{ on unfair die}) = \frac{2}{15} \times \frac{1}{6}$

Simplifies to: $\frac{1}{90} = \frac{1}{45}$

Question 25: D

The homeostatic response brings the level back to the stable, normal level. If the system is less responsive, all phases are likely to occur later (not earlier) and the deviation from the normal level will be higher. Thus, phase 2 would be higher.

Question 26: E

The key word here is **excess** oxygen. When sulphur reacts with oxygen, the product is Sulphur dioxide. This eliminates options A-C.

Since there is excess oxygen, the other product will be carbon dioxide (not carbon monoxide). Thus, E is correct.

Question 27: B

50 beats per minute means there is a beat every $\frac{6}{5}$ seconds. Since the back soldiers put down their left foot at the same time as the front soldiers put down their right, the adjusted beat is every $\frac{3}{5}$ seconds.

Thus, the $minimum\ distance\ = \frac{3}{5} \times 330 = \frac{990}{5} = 198$ m

END OF SECTION

Section 3

"Democratic freedom means there should be no restriction on what may be said in public."

➤ Democracy allows power to be vested in the people; it perpetuates the idea of freedom, equality and liberty, and thus the right of expression including freedom of speech. This suggests there should be no restriction or intervention if someone wishes to express their opinion in a public setting.

➤ Freedom of speech does not necessarily remove all boundaries; a restriction on the proclamation of unwarranted, extreme and prejudiced ideas seems just.

➤ People generally believe what they hear from people that appear more 'powerful' than them. Giving misleading information to the public can be dangerous; for example, the freedom to preach that drink-driving is not a crime to a bar could endanger many.

➤ Complete freedom of speech allows those with extreme ideas to declare whatever they believe, which could be to the detriment of young, impressionable minds enticed by these opinions.

➤ There should be a limit if 'free speech' is inciting hatred. Discrimination against minorities, whether it is sexuality, race or even age, can cause friction, hatred and 'broken' societies that is against the very notion of a democratic society.

➤ A utilitarian stance appears fairest; the 'harm principle' postulates that the actions of individuals should only be limited to those that prevent harm to other individuals, and this appears a good balance between completely free speech and a restrictive stranglehold. A difference in opinion can and should be freely expressed, but it is explicable that hate speech, classified information, obscenity, etc. is regulated.

The art of medicine consists of amusing the patient while nature cures the disease.

➢ The author argues the point that medicine is an art, and suggests that physicians need qualities of empathy and compassion to help satisfy patients' worries and beliefs while nature takes its course to cure them over time.

➢ Although this statement may have been wholly true in the 18th century, nowadays medicine is an applied science and it is debatable whether the statement still has any implications for the doctors of today.

➢ Scientific knowledge now allows us to treat patients better or more quickly than nature. Drugs target specific biochemical or physiological systems in order to cure. The fact that clinical trials are double blind and tested against a placebo and require a statistically significant difference between the groups highlights that the active ingredient of a drug is having an effect greater than that of nature and the 'amusing' of a patient. Example of the swine flu pandemic in 2009; oseltamivir highly successful. Many infectious diseases through history are now effectively eradicated worldwide.

➢ However, placebo is much more effective than no treatment, suggesting that patients can seek comfort in the thought that they are being cared for by those who they believe have the knowledge and skill to do so.

➢ Example of the common cold – can only treat the symptoms and wait for the innate immune system to take control.

➢ Doctors must always use more than science; examples include the importance of teamwork, leadership and diagnosis where there is no scientific method except interacting with the patient (e.g. bipolar disorder and other psychiatric illnesses).

A scientific man ought to have no wishes, no affections - a mere heart of stone.

➤ Darwin tackles the issue of objectivity in science; the ability to remain unbiased and develop conclusions true to our empirical evidence rather than true to our beliefs. Wishes and affections greatly influence one's behaviour and hence, one's rationality.

➤ Within science there undoubtedly exists a facet which requires absolute removal of our wishes and affections. These traits could influence experiments and therefore could and render invalid the interpretations of these studies, which would be detrimental in our aim to dispel our own ignorance and further scientific knowledge. There are many examples of where passion and bias have blinded scientists to that which has been objectively proven. A famous example is Sir Fred Hoyle who rejected Hawking's presentation of the Big Bang Theory despite overwhelming evidence (cosmic microwave background) until his death.

➤ It can be dangerous to not show complete objectivity. An example is the case of Andrew Wakefield, the gentlemen who asserted the link between the MMR vaccine and the onset of autism, which resulted in the deaths of many children from measles, mumps and rubella. (AW falsified his results and subjected autistic subjects to unethical procedures to 'prove' that the MMR vaccine causes autism after being bribed by a law firm that was planning on suing the MMR vaccine company. After repeat experiments were performed and the results acquired were found to be completely different, AW's paper was withdrawn from the Lancet and he was struck off the medical register.) Sadly, the myth that MMR vaccines cause autism is still believed and herd immunity has not reached pre-scare levels. Scientists should thus welcome other scientists with different prejudices and preferences to follow what they have done to see if they get the same results through peer reviewing.

➤ But our objectivity is not intended to quash our biases and natural passion and yearning for a scientific outcome. On the contrary, objectivity very much allows us to be passionate for science because it prevents the passion from influencing the results. So why have passion at all? Passion, drive and intrigue are intrinsic to scientific discovery and enquiry. Without such qualities Fleming or Darwin might never have discovered antibiotics and evolution. Einstein has always asserted the importance of imagination over knowledge. One reason is that imagination and creativity allows for options for technological advances that were unplanned and unprecedented (e.g. Fleming).

➤ One could argue that this is oxymoronic, as if one is "a scientific man" this suggests they have an affection and wish to proceed with scientific method. Without our wishes and affections, there would be no driving force underpinning our desire to understand how the world works.

Veterinary pet care in the UK should be free at the point of delivery, as human care is.

➤ The argument is that, as sentient beings, animals should receive free healthcare like their human owners.

➤ Animals experience disease, pain and illness in the same manner that we do, and our experience with these should mean our empathy extends to the animal world. The mantra of public healthcare is essentially that everyone deserves the 'right' of healthcare, regardless of wealth, status and privilege. Should this not translate to animals that are often most vulnerable?

➤ For most owners, their pet is part of the family and they would do anything to protect them and ensure they stay healthy.

➤ This plan would reduce the number if abandoned pets whose owners were unable to afford veterinary care.

~ 208 ~

➤ One of the core responsibilities of pet ownership is that you should make sure that you can take care of them and can afford to pay for everything that they need for the entire duration of their lives. If one cannot afford veterinary care, then perhaps they should not have a pet. Anyway, taking out pet insurance is recommended to most owners.

➤ Public healthcare through the NHS is only possible in the UK because taxpayers contribute towards its funding. In the case of veterinary care, forcing non-pet owners to pay taxes towards other people's pets - essentially, for a service that they will not use - seems very unfair. However, we do pay for the healthcare of those who smoke, heavily drink or take part in extreme sports, which is similarly 'unfair' in the sense that they are much more likely to use the publically funded money than others. Owners may agree to pay a kind of specific owner tax.

➤ It is also possible that pet owners may take less responsibility for their pet's health if they know that they will not have to pay for veterinary care.

➤ It is hard to draw a line between how well we should treat animals relative to ourselves. It is clear that in general we treat ourselves as if we are 'above' animals in society; we eat them, we test on them and we exploit them. If we have the resources to keep them healthy, then they deserve to have free healthcare, but this may be at the expense of other resources that the majority of people find more important in a democratic society.

END OF PAPER

2012

Section 1

Question 1: D

10% of the population is 8628709 x 0.1 = 862870.9, and the only islands with less than this amount are Brosnan and Dalton. 20% of the area is 26315 x 0.2 = 5263; Brosnan has less than this amount and Dalton has more, so the answer is Dalton.

HINT: As only 1 answer can be correct, for the second part of this question it can be assumed that the higher value is above 20% and the lower value is below 20% without doing any exact workings.

Question 2: C

As it is preceded by the words '*based on these findings,*' it is fairly easy to determine that the main conclusion of the passage is "*pale-skinned people should be added to the list of those for whom vitamin D supplements are recommended by the government.*"

A could probably be argued as correct based on the passage with a lack of a better answer, but the conclusion above clearly mentions supplements which this answer does not. Furthermore, the use of the word 'need' immediately suggests that the answer is probably too strong and thus incorrect.
B is probably true based on the information, but again is a point made to back up the argument rather than the main conclusion of the passage.
C paraphrases the conclusion given above, and is clearly the best answer.
D may be tempting from your previous knowledge, but is irrelevant and beyond the scope of this passage as skin cancer is not mentioned.
E is not correct as the passage makes no comparison between pale and dark skinned people. Again, we can probably rule this answer out from the start for being too strong and sweeping.

Question 3: F

The best way to answer this question is probably by using the process of elimination and testing the effect of removing each tile. Checking whether the number of black and white tiles is equal first is probably easiest as they stand out, but if this criterion is satisfied the other patterns must be checked too.

By removing A, you can see that you will be left with 6 black tiles and only 4 white tiles.
Removing B leaves 5 black tiles but 6 white tiles.
Removing C leaves 3 black tiles but 5 white tiles.
Removing D leaves 6 black tiles and only 5 white tiles.
Removing E leaves 5 black tiles and 5 white tiles. However, only 3 of the dotted pattern remain.
Removing F leaves 5 black tiles and 5 white tiles. It can also be seen that all the other patterns amount to 5 tiles.

Question 4: B

This question asks for a conclusion of the passage. A can be inferred but is not a conclusion of the passage.

B is the best answer as it sums up one of the fundamental points of the argument, "*only fossil fuels, which produce emissions of CO_2, can provide the extra capacity.*"
The use of the word 'never' in C immediately suggests that this is the incorrect answer, and there is no mention of the future potential of wind power.
D is incorrect, as the first sentence states that electric engines are more economical than petrol engines.

Question 5: E

The best way to answer this question is to work out the collective area of the shrubs, veg, pond and lawn, take this away from the total area and then determine the number of slabs needed. We are given several widths and heights of these areas and must work out the other ones.

The height of the pond is equal to the shrubs (3m), so the area of the pond is $3 \times 3 = 9m^2$.
The total width of the veg areas is $18 - 1 - 3 - 1 - 0.5 - 0.5 - 1 = 11$, and the total area of these plots are $11 \times 3 = 33m^2$.
The total width that the shrubs take up is $18 - 1 - 3 - 1 - 0.5 - 1 = 11.5m$, thus the total area that the shrubs take up is $4 \times 11.5 = 46m^2$.
The height that the lawn takes up is $12 - 1 - 3 - 1 - 1 = 6m$, so the area of the lawn is $3 \times 6 = 18cm^2$.
The total area of the garden is $18 \times 12 = 216m^2$, so the area taken up by the patio and paths is $216 - 9 - 33 - 46 - 18 = 110m^2$.
$1m^2$ requires 4 ($0.5m^2$) slabs, so $110m^2$ requires $110 \times 4 = 440$ slabs.

Question 6: E

The main conclusion of the argument is *"if parents spend time discussing these issues with their children they will help their children read well,"* given away by the use of the word 'so' and the fact that it is at the end of the passage. Flaws are generally related to the conclusion of the passage, whereas questions asking for statements that 'weaken' the argument could potentially relate to any of the passage.

A is clearly wrong as there is no mention of peer groups in the passage, and the statement has nothing to do with the conclusion above.
B could be maybe be debated, but appears like a weak suggestion in the face of other flaws given, and is not directly related to the conclusion of the argument.
C again could maybe be argued, but is again not linked to the conclusion of the argument, and there is clearly a more pertinent answer.

D is unrelated to the conclusion and is beyond the scope of the passage.
E is the best answer, as it directly addresses the conclusion above. A key principle in scientific argument, and hence the BMAT, is that correlation ≠ causation, which this statement asserts.

Question 7: A

This is a very difficult question, and you should ensure that you do not spend over 2 minutes trying to work this out and drawing all the permutations. For pattern questions like this it is best to work out what the repeating unit is (what you must add to carry on repeating the pattern indefinitely). This repeating unit consists of 1 hexagon, 2 triangles and 3 squares.

The easy way to do this was to realise that there are more squares than triangles in the diagram- this allows you to eliminate B,C and D. Intuitively, it is unlikely to be E (as that is obtained just by counting all the shapes)- leaving you with A as the only option.

Question 8: C

In questions like this it is too time-consuming to work with exact numbers and the best method is to work with close estimates. The total number of patient days we are dealing with is 11549 + 30432 = around 42000.

Method 1: The rate of infection is 9.86 per 10000 over ~30000 patient days, so over ~40000 days it will be ¾ of this value, which is slightly under 7.5, and 7.15 appears a very reasonable answer.

Method 2: There are 3 cases in 42000 days. To make this per 100000 days we have to times the number of cases by roughly. This equals 7.5 and again 7.15 appears the correct solution.

Question 9: D

The highest number of cases by far comes from organisation 3, with 26. This is out of a total of 69 (you can probably work this out using mental maths to save time). 26/69 is not intuitive, so we can use short division to work out that the first 3 digits are 0.37, suggesting that 38% is the correct answer of the ones listed.

HINT: we know that 69/3 is 23, thus 23/69 is equivalent to 1/3 or 33%. Our answer is higher than this value so we can easily rule out answers A-C.

Question 10: B

Again, don't waste time by working out exact values and use rough estimates.

Organisation 2 had 16000/11 = ~1500 patient days per month up to November, giving a total of 17500 for the year. We thus have 1 case in 17500 days but we need a value per 100000 days. 100000/17500 = 100/17.5.

100/17.5 is clearly between 5 and 6 as we know 100/5 = 20 and 100/6 = 16.7. This is an easy way of ruling out C-E.

We must then determine whether A or B is correct. We can work out that 17.5 x 5 = 87.5 and 17.5 x 6 = 105. 100 is closer to the latter, which means the answer is above 5.5 and thus must be 5.67.

Question 11: E

Is the correct answer, which we can determine by ruling out all of the other statements.

A & C - Several of the organisations are made up of more than 1 type of hospital, and the data is not split between these so we don't know which type of hospital the cases were found in. We can thus not reliably conclude where these Cdl cases occurred.

B - There is only 1 organisation with a small hospital alone, and this had only 1 case over 2009 and 2010 with a low rate of infection, so this is definitely incorrect.

D - Again, using the reasoning above, there may not necessarily have been any Cdl found in either DCs or TCs. For example, only organisation 5 has a DC in the data given and here, all the cases may have arisen from the TC.

Question 12: B

Nicola wants to get the first bus of the day from the airport, which is at 09:15 on Thursday. It takes 50 minutes to get to the centre, so she will be there at 10:05. She must get the 15:20 bus from the centre to reach the airport before 17:00. Thus she is in the centre between 10:05 to 15:20, which is 15:20 - 10:05 = 5 hours and 15 minutes.

Question 13: D

Reading the answers alone, the correct answer can probably be determined, as the other statements are far too strong and sweeping.
A uses the word 'only' and C uses the word 'must' which suggests they are wrong, and the passage is much less bold than these statements.
B is slightly less strong but the use of 'would not have' means the answer is not necessarily true, especially with a better answer present.
D is not overly strong and paraphrases the first sentence, making it the best answer.

Question 14: D

The cube must be visualised to work out this question. A and B can be ruled out because the triangle should always point to the long end of a solid line. C and E are excluded by looking at the configuration of the X and the surrounding shapes. If you get stuck and have time, make the net yourself – it will save time in the long run.

Question 15: C

The conclusion of this argument is *"parents of children with autism are damaging their children's health by using the sprays,"* and the rest is background information.

A would actually support this conclusion and does not weaken the argument

B would again strengthen the argument as it reinforces the idea that parents are potentially damaging children if preliminary tests have not been done.

C is the best answer, as if it were true, the claim in the conclusion becomes much less valid.
D isn't directly relevant to the question and doesn't potentially weaken the argument depending on what these cultural effects entail and is therefore not the right answer.
E also strengthens the argument by suggesting that oxytocin is bad.

Question 16: C

To make this question easier, we can focus on $1/6^{th}$ of the conservatory as it represents the pattern of the whole area. There are 25 tiles in this area, of which 5 have the pattern with no black, 4 have the pattern with ¼ black, 12 have the pattern which is ½ black and 4 have the pattern with all black. To work out the proportion of black, we need to work out the number of black tiles that these tiles add up to, and divide it by the total number of tiles. 0 x 5 + 0.25 x 4 + 0.5 x 12 + 1 x 4 = 11, and dividing this by 25 (times by 4 and divide by 100) is 0.44 (44%).

Question 17: G

None of the statements can be drawn as a conclusion of the passage. 1 - This is a strong statement and although the passage states staffing levels are lower at weekends and there are more deaths at weekends, it does not suggest the causation that increased staffing would reduce death rates.

2 – The passage states that patients are dying in hospitals rather than at home (which implies that they would die anyway). This artificially inflates the mortality stats. Thus, enhancing weekend provision of primary care services wouldn't help mortality rates- only massage the statistics.

3 - This again assumes the causation that low staffing levels leads to patient deaths, which is not what the passage suggests.

Question 18: A

If x is the percentage of people that own both a tumble dryer and a dishwasher, we must work out the smallest and largest possible values of x.

75to85 - x is the number of people with only a dishwasher, 35to40 - x is the number of people with only a tumble dryer, 0to5 is the number of people with neither and x is the number of people with both. Thus 75to85 - x + 35to40 - x + x + 0to5 = 100, meaning x = 75to85 + 35to40 + 0to5 - 100.

Smallest value: x = 75 + 35 + 0 - 100 = 10%, largest value: x = 85 + 40 + 5 = 30%

Question 19: B

The number of category A calls in 2011 was 2.23 million. 74.9% (we can take this as 75%) were responded to within 8 minutes, leaving 25% not responded to within 8 minutes. 2.23 x 0.25 is slightly above 0.5, and working it out fully gives an answer of 0.5575.

Question 20: D

We are told that category A calls made up around 34%, category B calls made up roughly 40% and so category C calls made up the remainder (26%). We thus want a pie chart showing Category C taking up very slightly more than a quarter of the graph and category A taking up around a third. Only pie chart D fits this bill.

Question 21: B

Is the only reasonable answer.

A is completely irrelevant to how many calls led to treatment/transport at the scene.
C suggests that something being a 'genuine emergency' completely determines whether people are treated/transported at a scene, which is not the   case.   B   is   the   better   answer.
D is wrong as category C cases may still require treatment/transport, but with different timings. Also, 26% of calls were category C, which amounts to over 2 million.

Question 22: A

In 2010, 2.08 million incidents were category A, and ~75% were attended within 8 minutes. 2.08 x 0.75 = 1.56m
In 2011, 2.23 million incidents were category B, and ~75% were attended within 8 minutes. 2.23 x 0.75 = 1.68m
1.68 - 1.56 = 0.12 million

Question 23: B

Working horizontally, we can see that patterns 1, 3, 8 and 10 are equivalent, patterns 6, 7 and 11 are equivalent and patterns 4 and 12 are equivalent. This leaves patterns 2, 5 and 9. 2 and 9 are equivalent through rotation, but pattern 5 cannot be rotated to match either of these. There are thus 5 distinct patterns.

Question 24: E

The conclusion is clearly the first line: "*Police should be given clear permission to use water cannons against rioters and rules about when it is appropriate.*"

A weakens the argument as it suggests that water cannons also affecting the innocent means it is not a good solution for targeting crime.
B could be debated as the answer, but the police are hardly against the use of training and resources.
C weakens the arguments as it suggests there are other equally useful strategies.
D mentions the high expense of water cannons and thus weakens the argument.
E is the best answer based on the information given, as it strengthens the idea that water cannons should be used.

Question 25: C

We can work out that the highest score in a full turn is 18 and the lowest is 2, which gives 17 possible scores. We must then work out if any scores between 2 and 18 are not possible (and we only need one example of a score being possible).

2 - 2, 2, miss.
3 - 2, miss, 2
4 - 4, 4, miss
5 - 4, 6, miss

The rest of the even numbers can be made with combinations of 2, 4 and 6

7 - 6, miss, 4
9 - 6, miss, 6
Higher odd numbers cannot be made, leaving 13 possibilities in total.

Question 26: D

This argument makes the reasoning error of x is z, y is z so z is x. There may be cases of z that are not x, or z may not link to x at all.

A follows x is y and y is z so x is z, which is reasonable.

B suggests x is y and z so everything z is y, which is wrong but a different error to that in the passage
C suggests x is y so not-x is not-y, which is (generally) fairly reasonable and definitely different to the reasoning error in the argument.
D follows x is z and y is z so x is z, which is the same reasoning argument as above.

Question 27: C

We know that furniture costs 3 months to pay, with ½ paid in the 1st month, and ¼ in the next 2 - this means that it does not matter whether sales of e.g. $2000 came from 1 sales or from several sale, as the money received per month will be equivalent in either case. We also know that there were no sales in May and June. Using these 2 pieces of information we can deduce the answer.

June must have been the final payment for 1 piece/pieces of furniture due to the closure, which means $2000 must also have come in from this April sale in May and $4000 in April. This gives a total of $8000 of sales from April The extra $1000 in April and May earned must have come from a sale in March, which would have amounted to a total of $4000 in March, and a total of $2000 earned from this/these sales in March.

The $2000 missing from March must have come from January sales of $8000, giving $4000 in January and $2000 in February. Any excess money from January and February must have come from furniture sold before January.
Thus the total sales in this time period are $8000 (January), $4000 (March) and $8000 (April), giving an answer of $20000.

~ 221 ~

Question 28: G

All the answers identify a weakness in the argument.

1. This is a weakness as saying *"this is nonsense"* suggests that the author thinks the ski holiday industry does not damage the environment, because all travel damages the environment.
2. This is a weakness as the argument that ski holiday resorts use less energy than other resorts is conflicted by this information. Using percentages here may mask the fact that absolute levels of energy consumption may be high, which this statement addresses
3. This is definitely a weakness as the author fails to consider that damage to the environment is not only caused by energy consumption.

Question 29: C

£12240 was made from y sales.
0.4y represents 40% of the ticket sales that were refunded £5 each.
So 0.6y x 20 + 0.4y x 15 = 12240. Solving for x gives x=680.
40% of 680 is 272 tickets, and £5 x 272 = £1360 refunded.

Question 30: C

Only statement 3 can be inferred. This could maybe be determined without the passage as it is least bold statement.
1 - *"authors…give a one sided view"* is very strong and the passage does not mention effectiveness or safety.
2 - There is nothing to suggest that *"companies…aim to influence the content of the articles."*
3 - This effectively paraphrases what is said in the first 2 sentences of the passage.

Question 31: C

We can deduce several things from this passage:

We know Jill must be at least 7 points ahead of 4th place so that even if she comes last and they come first the places remain the same. With the same reasoning, she must also be at least 7 points behind 2nd place.

Karen and Gemma must have the same number of points, so that even if one comes 3rd and one comes 4th, the final race determines who finishes on top.
The person in 4th place must have 7 points less than Jill if he is going to finish last (regardless of the scores in the last round).
The easiest way to do this is go through each option and see if the scores sum to 90. However, remember that 4th place gets 6 points in the last round so we need to take away 6 from each answer.
Option E: 23 – If 4th place has 23 in round 10, they have 17 in round 9. Thus, Jill has 24 in round 9 and the rest have 31 each. This sums to 103. [Too high]
Option D: 21 – If 4th place has 21 in round 10, they have 15 in round 9. Thus, Jill has 22 in round 9 and the rest have 29 each. This sums to 95. [Too high]
Option C: 19 – If 4th place has 19 in round 10, they have 13 in round 9. Thus, Jill has 20 in round 9 and the rest have 27 each. This sums to 87. [Close enough!]

Question 32: A

This question can be worked out relatively quickly without determining exact values. There were 7000 people killed out of 2.3 million vehicles in 1930, and 3180 people killed out of 27 million today. There are roughly half the people killed for 10 times the number of vehicles, which gives a fraction of 1/20, or 0.04 times as much.

Question 33: D

It is important to read exactly what the question is asking you here. It wants reasons that are *not already in the text* which strengthen the case for roads become safer.
A and C don't mean that roads are safer; if anything, it could mean that accidents are being under-reported (as mentioned in the article).

B and E are valid points but are mentioned in the article already.
D is a reasonable answer and gives us more of a reason to trust figures given in the article.

Question 34: C

This is probably the easiest question on the paper, and requires you to work out 40% of 319928. As the answer is wanted to the nearest 1000 anyway, 40% of 320000 is a reasonable calculation, which is 128000.

Question 35: A

Although a very strong statement, it is the only answer that is plausible based on elimination and accounts for the discrepancy in the results.
B is irrelevant, as roads being safer is unrelated to the discrepancy.
C would mean that hospital admissions decrease, but they remain unchanged.
D would mean the DfT figures should be higher than hospital figures.
E would again make DfT figures higher than the hospital.

END OF SECTION

Section 2

Question 1: F

Homeostasis is defined as the maintenance of constant internal conditions. Homeostatic responses occur whether a factor rises or reduces, and internal body conditions can be affected by changes in variables inside our body (e.g. blood glucose levels) or changes in variables in the environment (e.g. temperature). Thus, all the statements could result in a homeostatic response.

Question 2: D

Atomic mass of bromobutane = $(12 \times 4) + (9 \times 1) + 80 = 137g/mol$
Atomic mass of butanol = $(12 \times 4) + (10 \times 1) + 16 = 74g/mol$
Since the molar ratio between bromobutane and butanol is 1:1, we can form: $\frac{2.74}{137} = \frac{x}{74}$ where x is the theoretical yield.
Rearranging gives: $x = \frac{2.74 \times 74}{137} \approx \frac{3 \times 70}{140}$
$x = 1.5$ g.
The actual yield is 1.1g. Therefore, percentage yield = $\frac{1.1}{1.5} \times 100 = 73.3\%$
Note that because we rounded earlier on to make the maths easier, the answer isn't exactly 75%. This, is fine because the options are far enough apart to make **D** the only obvious answer. Remember, to **look at the options first to see how freely you can round numbers.**

Question 3: B

The first step is α decay, as 2 protons are lost, giving R-2. This means 2 neutrons are also lost, meaning the atomic mass is decreased by 4. The second step is β decay, so a neutron changes into a proton (plus an electron). This leaves the atomic mass unchanged as seen and the atomic number increases by 1. Thus, P = N – 4 and Q = R - 1

Question 4: A

There is no quick way to do this. Shaded Area $=$

Largest Circle + 2nd largest circle - 3rd Largest Circle - Smallest Circle

$$= \pi \left(\frac{4d}{2}\right)^2 + \pi \left(\frac{2d}{2}\right)^2 - \pi \left(\frac{3d}{2}\right)^2 - \pi \left(\frac{d}{2}\right)^2$$

$$= \pi [4d^2 + d^2 - \frac{9d^2}{4} - \frac{d^2}{4}]$$

$$= \pi [5d^2 + - \frac{10d^2}{4}]$$

$$= \pi d^2 [5 - 2.5]$$

$$= \frac{5}{2} \pi d^2$$

Question 5: B

1. Nicotine acts at the nicotinic acetylcholine receptors in the brain, leading to addiction.
2. Bronchitis is an infection of the bronchi, which can be caused by smoking and the bronchi is what area 2 points to.
3. Emphysema is a disease causing damage to the alveoli in the lungs, making you short of breath, and can be caused by smoking.
4. Carbon monoxide can enter your blood stream via the alveoli due to the effects of smoking.

Question 6: C

Lecithin is an emulsifier which has a hydrophilic head forming bonds with water and a hydrophobic tail forming bonds with oil, to prevent separation.

Question 7: F

None of the radiation is stopped by the paper, suggesting there is no α radiation. Some of the radiation is stopped by aluminium, but not all of it, suggesting the presence of β and γ radiation.

NB: Don't confuse yourself by bringing background radiation into this – the question strongly implies that it's not relevant here e.g. detector is **close** to the radioactive source.

Question 8: E

Remember to take a step by step approach when rearranging formulae:

$$G = 5 + \sqrt{7(9 - R)^2 + 9}$$

$$G - 5 = \sqrt{7(9 - R)^2 + 9}$$

$$(G - 5)^2 = 7(9 - R)^2 + 9$$

$$\frac{(G-5)^2 - 9}{7} = (9 - R)^2$$

$$9 - R = \sqrt{\frac{(G-5)^2 - 9}{7}}$$

$$R = 9 - \sqrt{\frac{(G-5)^2 - 9}{7}}$$

Question 9: A

The patient will no longer be able to sense pain if these neurons cannot detect stimuli normally causing pain.
Statement 1 must be correct as it is involved in each answer. There would be no reflex response if the neuron does not sense any pain.
Statement 2 is correct. If there is a visual stimulus, such as a pin prick coming towards you, then you would still move away based on vision alone.
Statement 3 and 4 suggest that the patient can sense the pain but this is incorrect.

Question 10: D

It is easier to use an elimination method rather than trying to balance this equation manually. Start by balancing for Phosphorous, as it has relatively simple values in the equation. The quickest way to do this is via algebra (for more information, see the Chemistry chapter in *The Ultimate BMAT Guide*).

For Phosphorous: $A + B = 3C$;
Only Options C + D fulfil this equation. Thus, we can eliminate, A, B + E.
Next, for Hydrogen: $2A + B = 2D$; Only D fulfil this equation.

Question 11: D

For work to be done, a force must act in a parallel direction to the object.

1. The person sat on the chair hasn't moved so no work has been done.
2. The force is acting perpendicular to the direction of motion. Thus, whilst work is being done to move the barrow, $Work\ done \neq Fd$.
3. d represents the direction in which work is being done so $Work\ done = Fd$

Question 12: E

$$= \sqrt[3]{\frac{2 \times 10^5}{(5 \times 10^{-3})^2}} - \sqrt{4 \times 10^3 - 4 \times 10^2}$$

$$= \sqrt[3]{\frac{2 \times 10^5}{25 \times 10^{-6}}} - \sqrt{4000 - 400}$$

$$= \sqrt[3]{\frac{2 \times 10^5}{2.5 \times 10^{-5}}} - \sqrt{3600}$$

$$= \sqrt[3]{0.8 \times 10^{10}} - 60 = \sqrt[3]{8 \times 10^9} - 60$$

$$= 2 \times 10^3 - 60$$

$$= 2000 - 60$$

$$= 1940$$

Question 13: E

Answer 1 could be an explanation as the antibiotic discs Q and R have very similar effects on the bacterial colonies. Answer 2 is unrelated to the question and the fact that the antibiotic is working suggests there is little to no resistance. Answer 3 is potentially correct as this is where the distance up to which the bacteria are destroyed.

Question 14: F

As all of the possible formulae of azurite have 3 copper atoms, we know the stoichiometry of the reaction is 2 of one of the reagents and 1 of the other. We can test both of these combinations.

$2CuCO_3 + Cu(OH)_2 \rightarrow Cu_3C_2H_2O_8$ which is as a possible answer.

$CuCO_3 + 2Cu(OH)_2 \rightarrow Cu_3CH_4O_7$ which is not a possible answer.

Question 15: B

$Wave\ speed\ =\ frequency\ x\ wavelength$

$f = \frac{3\ x\ 10^8}{0.12}$, so f = 2.5 x 10^9 Hz

As frequency stays constant, wavelength = $\frac{2.0\ x\ 10^8}{2.5\ x\ 10^9}$ = $0.08\ m = 8cm$

Question 16: C

There are several ways of doing this question. One of the simples is to form additional triangles by adding a point on the line MB.

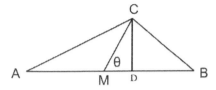

$Tan\ (x) = \frac{opposite}{adjacent}$ and since:

➢ Tan B= 2/3 ➔ CD = 2 and DB = 3.
➢ Tan A = 1/6 ➔ Since, CD is 2, $AD = 2\ x\ 6 = 12$
➢ $AB = AD + DB = 12 + 3 = 15$

Then, looking at right angled triangle CMD, we know the opposite length is 2 and the adjacent length can be calculated as follows:

Since, M is the midpoint, $MD = 7.5 - DB = 4.5$

Therefore $Tan\ \theta = \frac{2}{4.5} = \frac{4}{9}$

Question 17: C

It is helpful to write out the relationship described:

Alcohol ➔ ADH decreases ➔ Dilute Urine produced. Thus, we can conclude that ADH concentrates urine.

1 is correct as all hormones travel in the bloodstream. There is a negative correlation between dilute urine production and ADH levels, rendering 2 and 3 incorrect. 4 is correct as increased formation of dilute urine means more water is lost and dehydration may occur.

Question 18: D

This requires you to have memorised the reactivity series. Zinc, and thus vanadium, are below Chlorine, Sodium, aluminium and magnesium in the reactivity series so they can be displaced by the more reactive elements. However, Zinc and vanadium are above iron in the reactivity series. Thus, the less reactive iron will not be able to displace the more reactive vanadium from a compound.

Question 19: D

Consider each factor in turn:

➢ Total resistance: The circuit changes from parallel to a series which have a higher overall resistance.
➢ Ammeter 1 measures overall current. Since, total resistance has increased, and the voltage is the same, the total current must decrease in accordance with Ohm's Law (V = IR).
➢ Ammeter 2 was measuring the current in a branch. Since, the circuit is now in series, the current no longer 'splits' at branches. Thus, the entire current flows through ammeter 2. Therefore the current flowing through this ammeter will increase.

Question 20: B

The balls are arranged to give the smallest possible probability for the player to win. Thus, the arrangement is:
➢ Bag 1: 2 red and 2 yellow
➢ Bag 2: 2 red, 1 yellow and 1 blue

There are 3 ways to win, each with equal probability:
➢ 2 yellows from bag 1
➢ 2 reds from bag 1
➢ 2 reds from bag 2

The probability of any choosing the correct bag = ½

Thus, the probability of picking the above permutations is given by:
$$= \frac{1}{2} \; x \frac{2}{4} \; x \frac{1}{3} = \frac{1}{12}$$

Since, there are 3 ways of winning, the probability of winning $= \frac{1}{12} \; x \; 3 \; = \frac{1}{4}$

Question 21: D

Statement 1 is wrong, as this does the opposite of explaining why there are less recessive phenotypes than expected. The other 2 reasons are correct and are fundamental ideas in scientific research (we need large sample sizes to reduce the effect of chance).

Question 22: B

This is easier than it looks. Remember that Helium is an inert gas so HeOH is not a plausible product. Tritium beta decays to a single Helium atom. Thus, Let T represent both Helium and Tritium in the equations below:

HTO → $H_2O + O_2 + T$ or   HTO → $H_2O + H_2 + T$

The first equation can be balanced as: 4HTO → $2H_2O + O_2 + 4T$ but the second equation cannot be balanced. Thus, the only possible products are those shown by option 2.

Question 23: D

$Loss\ in\ E_p = mg\Delta h = 100\ x\ 10\ x\ 100 = 10^5 J$

Since the cyclist descends 100m vertically, and for every 1m descended 10m is travelled along the road, the cyclist travels 1000m along the road.

Since Work is being done by the cyclist: Work Done = Force x Distance

Therefore, $Force = \frac{10^5}{10^3} = 10^2 N$

Since the cyclist is travelling at constant velocity, the resultant force must = 0. Thus: Resistive Force = Force due to weight = 100 N.

Question 24: A

This is a tough question:

➤ Let the cost of wood be y, and the cost of metal 3y
➤ Let the quantity of metal used be m_1, which is proportional to d
➤ Let the quantity of wood used be w_1, which is proportional to d^2
➤ Total Cost=$3y \times m_1 + y \times w_1$

Now we have 2d:
$m_2 = 2d = 2m_1$
$w_2 = (2d)^2 = 4d^2 = 4w_1$
3(total cost) = $3y \times m_2 + y \times w_2 = 6y \times m_1 + 4y \times w_1$
Substitute for total cost: $3(3y \times m_1 + y \times w_1) = 6y \times m_1 + 4y \times w_1$
$9m_1 + 3w_1 = 6m_1 + 4w_1$
$3m_1 = w_1$
Percentage of metal = $m_1/(m_1+w_1) = \frac{1}{4} = 25\%$

Question 25: E

It is easiest to work backwards in each case.

Let's call the dominant allele A and the recessive allele a. Remember we are looking for the **minimum number**. When only U is recessive (aa), S and T must be heterozygous (Aa). If one was dominant, then they would not be able to produce offspring with the recessive condition.

R can be AA. Only one of P or Q must be Aa so that S is also heterozygous, giving a total of 3. When R is also recessive, P and Q must be heterozygous, along with S and T, giving a total of 4 heterozygous individuals.

~ 233 ~

Question 26: E

$C_2H_4 + H_2 \rightarrow C_2H_6$

The pressure will initially increase due to the increase in temperature. However, the final pressure will be ½ of the initial pressure because:
➤ Pressure is determined the number of moles of a gas present and
➤ The products have ½ the number of moles as the reactants.

Question 27: G

➤ Statement P is wrong as the speed of sound is constant in air (330 m/s).
➤ Q is wrong because the amplitude would be half of the distance between X and Y (2.5 mm)
➤ R is wrong because we cannot comment on wavelength with the available data.
➤ Frequency $= \dfrac{1}{0.2 \; x \; 10^{-3}} = 1,000 \; x \; 5 = 5 \; kHz$.
➤ Thus, only statement S is correct.

END OF SECTION

Section 3

"Doubt is not a pleasant condition, but certainty is absurd." (Voltaire)

➤ Voltaire suggests that whilst questioning something can be a very daunting feeling it is better than merely accepting something as certain. This statement therefore encapsulates the concept of science, where every idea and theory can be challenged and questioned. Many theories that have previously been accepted as 'truth' in the past are later revised. Doubt is at least a logical position where one can look for more answers and evidence.

➤ It can be argued that some things are 'certain' and are not necessarily absurd. At school we are taught that it is certain that the sun will rise tomorrow, and there has never been evidence to suggest otherwise. Of course, there is the miniscule possibility of a cataclysmic event, which would have to consist of something beyond our current knowledge of physics. However, does this factor mean it is 'absurd' to declare the sun rising as a certainty? Other things that seem certain include the fact that we are all currently living, and that somebody who is deceased will not come back to life.

➤ Good statement to promote scientific, rational and logical thinking scientific, but absurd may be too strong a word.

"There is something attractive about people who don't regard their own health and longevity as the most important things in the world." (Alexander Chancellor)

➢ This statement describes admiration for those who are unselfish and consider others needs as much as theirs. The chancellor condemns living egocentrically, whereby one is concerned only for prolonging their life and well-being.

➢ It can be argued that one's own health and longevity is more important than anything else; ultimately we are biological creatures who must undergo survival of the fittest in the evolutionary process of natural selection and thus our main aim is to preserve our genetic information, meaning our fitness is more important than other's fitness. We must compete with others and this involves placing ourselves above others. If we were to ignore this self-worth and put others above us, then we may also end up suffering. We only live once, and in that sense one's health and life can be regarded as highly precious (as its virtually irreplaceable) and therefore it should have the highest worth other others or material possessions.

➢ It is very humanitarian to consider other people's health and longevity; this can be through religious influences, or through 'humanist' principles. These argue that as a human race we should value each other's survival as a whole; that is perhaps a factor why we have progressed through the ages and seen this openness gradually accepted as a social norm today. Altruistic behaviour, empathy and many other traits based on selflessness are arguably what make us 'human'.

The scientist is not someone who gives the right answers but one who asks the right questions.

➤ The statement addresses the argument that science is not just about reading textbooks, memorizing info and regurgitating it when necessary; it is instead about asking the pertinent questions that allow scientific advancement.

➤ Scientists must be comfortable with the unknown to allow progression; they want to have answers to find, rather than needing answers to everything.

➤ A scientist cannot formulate satisfactory answers without satisfactory questions; a fundamental principle of scientific research is that a hypothesis, derived from a scientific question, must be present before any experimentation takes place.

➤ Science is about thinking "How does that work", or "why does this happen", and then trying to answer that question. Some of the most exciting science discoveries would never have happened, without that initial spark of inspiration from an inquisitive question. If Newton hadn't asked himself how the apple came to fall to Earth, or Darwin hadn't asked why the mockingbirds on different islands were separate species, could they possibly have found the answers to these questions?

➤ Insightful questions can challenge accepted models, and turn the way we think about a concept on its head. However, you still need a curious, inquisitive mind to come up with the right answers.

➤ Questions without answers are often frustrating and undesirable, suggesting the answer is at least as important as the question. Indeed, neuroscientists studying consciousness focus on the 'easy problems' which can be viably studied and avoid the 'hard problems' for which we do not even know how to approach to determine an answer.

> A scientific theory is empirical and is therefore always open to falsification. Accepted beliefs and conventions are changeable in science; what we believe to be true now could easily be disproved in 100 years, 50 years, or tomorrow. Inspiration for progression can come in several ways. It can come from realising that the old questions are no longer working, highlighting the importance of scientific questions. Or, it can come from thinking of new ways to approach old questions, and this represents innovation with the answer rather than the question.

> Einstein claimed "I have no special talents, I am just passionately curious."

"... Dolphins are very intelligent and so similar to humans that they are worthy of a special ethical status: that of 'non-human persons'."

> Dolphins have distinct personalities, self-awareness, forward thinking, complex social structures, empathy, and many other 'higher' functions we previously only attributed to humans. This has been shown through studies functionally and anatomically. The statement suggests that this should lead to the, having an ethical status of 'non-human persons' which will give them a legally enforceable right to life.

> Animals are generally all bound by equal animal rights, whereas humans are bound by equal human rights, and within these groups we do not differentiate for intelligence. Why should there be an exception for dolphins?

> We have no concept of what being a dolphin is like, as they live in a completely different environment and have different lifestyles. We currently mistreat them and should they not be protected from exploitation? (Although this also could apply to other animals)

> Intelligence is an extraordinary attribute, and the fact that they are self-aware and are likely to experience similar emotions in a similar way to us means it appears unethical to use them for our entertainment or kill them for food, suggesting they deserve these rights.

➤ Are there many downsides to giving dolphins rights? Most don't aim to kill them either deliberately or inadvertently, and there isn't much to lose. If they are sentient beings whose intelligence warrants such rights then it seems like a rational idea. All life is sacred, but arguably those with higher levels of consciousness deserve more respect and more protection.

➤ If an animal is more intelligence than another should it receive greater treatment? The notion because x is smarter than y then x should not be killed brings many ethical implications along with it.

➤ "Intelligent" behaviour of various kinds is found in many animals and when we measure intelligence, we do so according to a human (and culturally specific) norm. Even in testing human intelligence, there is controversy over these issues. Why should intelligence be the standard for conferring rights? Does this mean that mentally handicapped humans or those suffering from dementia should be denied rights? Then, there is a question as to whether these rights are to be extended to all cetaceans or only the most intelligent ones.

➤ One can support the protection of animals, but intelligence appears to be a rigid and possibly unjustified standard to use in order to decide which animals deserve what protection.

END OF PAPER

2013

Section 1

Question 1: A

This question can be worked out sequentially using the information given. Carla isn't working on Monday, which means Bob and Amy must be. That fills Bob quota of 3 days in the week. This means Carla and Amy must be working on Wednesday and Thursday. Amy cannot also work on Tuesday, as that would make it 4 consecutive days, so Carla must work on Tuesday too.

Question 2: C

A is a very bold statement and probably too strong to even be considered. The passage doesn't say that life can't exist on Kepler-22b and in fact even suggests that its new reclassification as uninhabitable may be inaccurate.

B suggests the opposite of the background we are given. Cosmologists now suggest that less planets are habitable than previously thought.
C summarises a main conclusion of the passage and is thus the best answer. The passage gives the example of Earth; that it is close to being outside the habitable zone but is robustly life-friendly, doubting the accuracy of the criteria.
D cannot be inferred from this information alone. The passage doesn't describe a link between clouds and Kepler-22b

Question 3: C

There are 6 combinations, and each one can be tested by determining the number of days between birthdays. If this equals a multiple of 7 then their birthdays are always on the same day of the week. 281 - 218 = 63, so Adam and Tara have their birthdays on the same day of the week every year.

Question 4: C

The main conclusion of the argument is easy to spot in this argument, as it is at the end of the passage and begins with the word 'therefore.'

A, B and D are points which are mentioned in the text, but only as background information and they do not constitute the conclusion of the passage.
C paraphrases the conclusion that *"the secret to losing weight is painfully simple - do more and/or eat less"* and is thus the best answer.

E is incorrect as the conclusion also describes that eating less can lead to calorie burn.

Question 5: D

Jason sold y Spruggles on day 1, and 2y on day 2. They cost £12 on day 1 and £9 on day 2, and he made £342 more on day 2. Thus y x 12 + 342 = 2y x 9. We want 3y (how many were sold altogether).
$18y = 12y + 342$
$6y = 342$
$3y = 171$

Question 6: C

The main point of the Clovis-First theory is that the Clovis were *the first inhabitants* of the Americas.
C is the only answer that would seriously challenge this point, as it has a specific time linked to it. The Clovis first theory suggests that they arrived at -11500 BC, and if there was a human settlement present 500 years before this time then this disproves the theory.
The other answers all link to the background information given, and could all be legitimate in a 'weaken' question, but none others seriously challenge that the Clovis were the first inhabitants.

Question 7: A

Although elimination may seem quite a long process on the surface, it can be done rather quickly.

Simon has 5 letters in his name so is limited to Hyde and Rush, and cannot be Rush because of the letter s. **Simon Hyde**

Liam has 4 letters in his name so is limited to Doyle, Floyd and Shore, and must be Shore because of the letter l. **Liam Shore**

Dylan has 5 letters in his name and must thus be Rush. **Dylan Rush**

Eric must be Doyle or Floyd. It cannot be Doyle due to the letter e. **Eric Floyd.** Thus Ian's surname must be Doyle. **Ian Doyle**

Question 8: D

D is clearly the correct answer, especially given that the question tells you that it is a sarcastic comment. If you find it hard to spot sarcasm, then we can rule out B and C as the comment links to the quote about children rather than the other 2, and the sarcasm of 'no' means we should agree with whatever the quote says, which is paraphrased in D.

Question 9: A

Answer A basically paraphrases this 'evidence' and is thus the correct answer. The statement does not relate to what wealth should bring, or anything about children. D assumes a causality which is not necessarily suggested by the statement.

Question 10: D

1. Kahneman suggests that the better you are at the job, the more time you must invest in it. However, this does not necessarily imply that people who work shorter hours will give more time to their children - they may use this 'extra' time in other ways.

2. The transcript talks about not getting happier as we get richer over a certain level. However, it does not suggest that wealth under this level will not cause stress.

~ 242 ~

Question 11: B

Anecdotal evidence is evidence based on personal accounts rather than facts or research, which this story clearly is. It is not necessarily conclusive without facts to back it up, there are no statistics and it is relevant. We can argue that it is not hearsay as it is said that she is intimately involved with the family she describes.

Question 12: B

BEWARE that the symbol for Mercury and the symbol for Venus/Copper look very similar.
We can use the process of elimination here.
We can start with the first card, and at the top. There is only 1 equivalent to moon, which is silver on card 4, but the second item is different, so we can rule out cards 1 and 4 for having a pair.
The second card has 3 equivalents for the top item - cards 6, 7 and 8. The second item is only equivalent for card 7, and the last item for cards 2 and 7 are different, thus we can rule out all these cards as having a pair.
We are left with cards 3 and 5, and we can see that these are equivalent. Thus we have 1 pair in total.

Question 13: D

The main conclusion of the argument is *"In the interests of providing the most desirable outcomes, it is clear that placebos should be used as a treatment offered by the NHS."* Thus, if treatments (such as placebos) ensure better outcomes, they should be used, which is paraphrased in D. A doesn't necessarily support the argument, as you do not know whether the placebo will work. B, C and E are unrelated to the fundamental point of the argument.

Question 14: B

We can start by ruling out 8 and 5, as this would break the alphabetical order rule.

Let's call the missing digits x and y. From the information given in the text, we know that $4 + 0 + x + y = 8$ + number of letters in x + number of letters in y. So $x + y = 4$ + number of letters in x and y.
Testing this rule out gives the exclusive answer of $x + y$ being 9 and 2. Here, it is important to re-read the question and make sure you give the number of letters that make up these digits, which is 7.

Question 15: B

A and C actually strengthen the argument as they back up some of the points made in the passage. D is a point against the argument, but doesn't weaken it, and is merely a statement saying the opposite of the passage. B is clearly the best answer as it directly contradicts the point that "*sport is what people do to counter the stress and pressures of work*" which is a key point in the author's argument that the growth of extreme sports is puzzling.

Question 16: C

It is useful to quickly jot down the first letter of each month on a rough sheet of paper. J F M A M J J A S O N D. You can then determine which months the birthdays can occur on, along with the number of the month in the year.
Jenny's and Alice's birthdays are 2 months apart - you can determine that this is only possible if Jenny's birthday is in June. It can't be in January or July because there would be no month 2 months away beginning with the letter A. Alice's birthday could be in August or April.
Alice's and Michael's birthdays are 5 months apart - you can determine that this is only possible if Alice's birthday is in August and Michael's is in March, using the same logic as above. Thus Jenny's birthday is in June, Michael's is in March, making them 3 months apart.

Question 17: D

This argument suggests that age makes us lack sleep and age makes us have impaired memory, so the lack of sleep must cause the impaired memory. This is an error of reasoning.

1 and 3 highlight different ways that these ideas may be connected, aside from lack of sleep causing impaired memory, highlighting weaknesses in the error of reasoning. 2 is unrelated to this error of reasoning and doesn't weaken the argument.

Question 18: B

Start by writing all the square numbers between 1 and 60. The month must be 09, the day can be between 1-30, the hour can be between 1-24 and the minute can be between 1-60.

There are 4 possible days: 1, 4, 16, 25. If we start with day 01, then there are 8 times: 4:16, 4:25, 4:36, 4:49, 16:04, 16:25, 16:36 and 16:49. There will be the same number of times for days 4 and 16, as you can have 2 different hours and 4 times per hour without including the same square number, giving 24 times from these particular days.

However, for day 25, there are more possible days, as you can have 3 different hours: 1, 4 and 16. These have 4 times per hour each, giving 12 times in total from this day.

$24 + 12 = 36$.

Question 19: B

There is no possible way that X can be green. The bottom left region must be green; it cannot be blue, yellow or red as there would be an edge with the same colour on both sides. The region to the top right of X can be red or yellow. When it is red, X can be yellow or blue. When it is yellow, X can be red or blue. Thus the region can be yellow, blue or red.

Question 20: C

If this circle was smaller than a square, and contained within a square, it could be the opposite colour to the square and no rules would be broken. If it was not contained within a square, or larger than a square, then it would have to be a different colour to the black and white to prevent any edge having the same colour on both sides.

Question 21: A

This is probably best done by trial and error. Try using 3 lines in many different combinations, and you will eventually see that 2 colours will always be sufficient, as a segment will never share an edge with more than 2 other segments, both of which can be the other colour.

Question 22: B

We can think of the top and bottom as 2 separate circles (or any shape) with 5 separate segments. If we look at the circles individually, we can see that 2 colours cannot suffice, as there would have to be 2 adjacent. 3 colours suffice. When we superimpose this on another circle, 3 colours are sufficient to never have 2 adjacent faces the same colour.

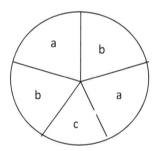 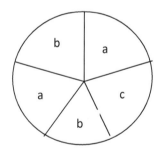

Question 23: D

Types of tile:
Fully black
½ black
¼ black
¾ black
Black line outlines ¼
Black line outlines ½

2 X Black line outlines ½, ¼ black - this may be the one that people miss, as there are 2 forms of this shape and one cannot be rotated to form the other. If in doubt, take a rough piece of paper, draw the shape and try rotating it to see whether the tiles are equivalent.

Question 24: B
The main conclusion of this article is that "*to reduce the harm done by alcohol, it is vital to reduce consumption.*" The author argues that one of the best ways to do this is to make alcohol more expensive. Answer B suggests that cheaper prices have led to more consumption of alcohol, backing up the point that alcohol consumption is based on price. Answer A is irrelevant to the point about reducing consumption and answers C and D do not strengthen the argument.

Question 25: B

The clocks are 41 minutes apart. The hour change must between 19 and 20. Within the same hour there would be the same digit used, or with the same first hour digit. 23 to 00 cannot be used as the 0 is used twice and 09 to 10 also uses the 0 twice. **19:ab and 20:cd** c cannot be 0, 1 or 2 as these numbers are already used. It cannot be 4 as cd could only be 40 or 41 (41 minutes apart), and the 0 and 1 digits have been used. This means c must be 3, and thus a is 5. **19:5b and 20:3d** b or d cannot be 1, 2, 3, 5 or 9 as these have been used. If b is 4, then d would have to be 5 which is not possible. b can be 6 or 7 and d can be 7 or 8. **19:56-19:57 and 20:37 and 20:38.** There is no 4 used here.

Question 26: A

There is no easy way to do this- if you struggle with spatial awareness then this would be extremely difficult. Number 5 makes contact with P followed by 7 onto Q, 4 onto R and 1 onto S.

Question 27: C

We know Al is married and Charles is unmarried. Beth could be married or unmarried. C is the correct statement, as one way or the other, there was someone married looking at someone unmarried.

Question 28: D

The argument is *against* the idea that children should be exposed to harsh realities from a young age. Only D supports this, whereas the others suggest the opposite.

Question 29: E

Again this was a difficult spatial awareness question and the only quick way to solve it would be to actually make the net in the exam. The rules don't explicitly state that you may not use scissors although you should certainly approve it with your exams officer before. If spatial awareness isn't your forte- this was certainly one question to skip.

Question 30: D

1 and 3 are fundamental principles of evolution, which can be assumed when the word evolution is used. The argument says *"this characteristic must have evolved because it gave human beings a better grip underwater"* and this would not have 'evolved' if it were not advantageous. 2 is true from our previous knowledge, but is irrelevant to the argument and does not need to be assumed at any point.

Question 31: A

First write down all the remaining numbers between 3 and 12, and cross each one out when used.

Bottom row: 10+12=22, so the other 2 numbers must be add up to 7 to make 29. This means they must be 3 and 4, although we do not yet know in which order.

Top row: 5+9=14, so the other 2 numbers must add up to 15. This can only be made from 7 and 8, although we do not yet know in which order. Right column: 11 must be above the 6, and we require 12 more. This means top right must be 8 and bottom right must be 4. This makes the person opposite 9 as 3.

Question 32: B

If 1% of non-cannabis users in the sample develop psychosis, and cannabis users were 41% more likely to have psychosis, 1.41% of cannabis users in the sample will have psychosis. 20% of young people report using cannabis, which is 2000 people. 2000 x 0.0141 = 2 x 14.1 = 28.2 users.

Question 33: A

Let's call the probability of psychosis for reasons other than cannabis use y. 80% of the population have probability y of getting psychosis, whereas 20% of the population have probability y plus the extra 41%.

We thus have 1.41 x 0.2y + 0.8y as the probability of getting psychosis, and the percentage of getting it through cannabis use is 0.41 x 0.2y/(1.41 x 0.2y + 0.8y)

Y cancels, and the top is roughly 0.08 and the bottom is slightly over 1, giving a percentage of slightly less than 8%, so A must be correct.

Question 34: B

The passage suggests that an increase in x (cannabis use) causes an increase in y (psychosis), whereas this answer provides an alternative link and suggests that y may also cause an increase in x. A mentions age but this is not an alternative reason for the link. C suggests that the link may not be valid, which is irrelevant to what the question is asking. D is a point against an alternative link, suggesting more psychotic patients may have used cannabis than we think.

Question 35: C

Causal link is the key phrase here, and is a common theme in science and thus the BMAT. We need some evidence that A to B may be more than just a correlation.

A may look tempting on the surface, but it again doesn't prove causation. There may be a separate causal factor which affects you when young or old that links to cannabis and psychosis, rather than the cannabis itself.
B, if anything, is against a direct causal link between cannabis and psychosis, highlighting that other factors may be involved.
C suggests a causal link, because an increase in X (cannabis strength) **caused** an increase in Y (psychosis).
D is irrelevant to showing a causal link.
E is irrelevant to showing a causal link.

END OF SECTION

Section 2

Question 1: H

Both the nervous system and the endocrine system are involved in homeostasis. Some of the messaging takes place using chemicals and they can receive and send messages to and from the brain.

Question 2: D

This refers to the reactivity series. A displacement reaction can take place if the element in the salt is lower down in the reactivity series than the element it is being reacted with. This only applies to 1 and 4, where Al and Zn and higher in the reactivity series than Pb and Cu respectively.

Question 3: D

Both 1 and 2 are correct in their ability to damage. However, infrared does not cause damage when penetrating matter.

Question 4: A

$$\frac{4.6 \times 10^7 + 7 \times 2 \times 10^6}{4.6 \times 10^7 - 2 \times 2 \times 10^6}$$

$$= \frac{4.6 \times 10^7 + 14 \times 10^6}{4.6 \times 10^7 - 4 \times 10^6}$$

$$= \frac{4.6 \times 10^7 + 1.4 \times 10^7}{4.6 \times 10^7 - 0.4 \times 10^7}$$

$$= \frac{6.0 \times 10^7}{4.2 \times 10^7}$$

$$= \frac{6}{4.2}$$

$$= \frac{60}{42}$$

$$= \frac{10}{7}$$

Question 5: F

Protease would break down proteins into amino acids; lipase would break down fats into fatty acids and therefore lower the pH of the solution. However, carbohydrase would function to break up the carbohydrates and would produce the non-acidic sugar products, therefore not lowering the pH.

Question 6: B

This reaction is in equilibrium, with the greater number of moles on the left hand side of the equation than the left. This means that an increase in pressure would push the equilibrium to the right, therefore producing more T product. In addition, since the forward reaction is exothermic, a lower temperature shifts the equilibrium towards the products. Catalysts have no effect on yield of product, just on reaction speed, and addition of more reactants would obviously increase the product yield.

Question 7: H

The switch being closed has turned the circuit from a series to parallel which therefore has a lower overall resistance. Since total voltage is unchanged, current must increase in accordance with V=IR. Thus P increases. With the switch open, the voltage is shared across both resistors but with it closed, the second resistor can be bypassed (short-circuited) by the new branch. This means that only the full voltage is shared by the first resistor only. Thus, Q increases and R decreases.

Question 8: F

$$4 - \frac{x^2(1-16x^2)}{(4x-1)2x^3} = 4 - \frac{(1-16x^2)}{2x(4x-1)}$$

Thus: $\frac{8x(4x-1)}{2x(4x-1)} - \frac{(1-4x)(1+4x)}{2x(4x-1)}$

$= \frac{8x(4x-1)}{2x(4x-1)} + \frac{(4x-1)(4x+1)}{2x(4x-1)}$

Thus: $\frac{8x}{2x} + \frac{(4x+1)}{2x}$

$= \frac{8x+4x}{2x} + \frac{1}{2x}$

$= 6 + \frac{1}{2x}$

Question 9: F

Sensory neurons are the longest types of neurons as they must travel all the way to the spinal cord. The relay neurons are the shortest because they are only present in the spinal cord.

Question 10: B

This involves the equation 2Na+ 2H$_2$O ➔ H$_2$ + 2NaOH. You can therefore work out the moles of sodium by using $Mass = moles \; x \; M_r$:
$Moles \; of \; Sodium = \frac{1.15}{23} = 0.5 \; moles$
Since the molar ratio between Sodium and hydrogen gas is 2:1, 0.25 moles of hydrogen are produced.
Therefore, Volume of Hydrogen = 22.4 x 0.25 = 5.6 dm^3 = 560 cm^3.

~ 253 ~

Question 11: C

Remember that:

> ➢ Angle of incidence < Critical Angle: Light Reflected Back
> ➢ Angle of incidence = Critical Angle: Total Internal Reflection
> ➢ Angle of incidence > Critical Angle: Light leaves outside

Diagram 1 is has an angle below the critical angle. Therefore, total internal reflection does not occur and instead the light is reflected out. In diagram 2, the angle is greater than the critical angle. Therefore, total internal reflection does not occur and instead the light passes through.

Question 12: B

Label the corners of the square as A, B C and D and then see where they move in relation to the transformations performed. A reflection in the y axis therefore leads to the original orientation.

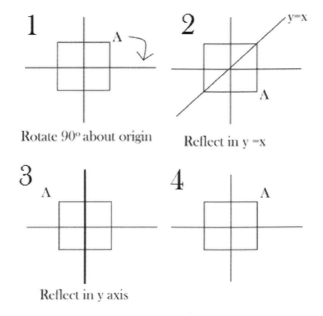

1 Rotate 90° about origin

2 Reflect in y =x

3 Reflect in y axis

4

Question 13: C

The actual protein is not needed to produce it, as the intention is to allow the bacteria to produce the protein from the implanted DNA.

Question 14: A

In $MgCl_2$, the 2 valence electrons in Mg will each go to a chlorine atom, which will then mimic a filled orbital. The chloride atoms will both have the same electronic structure as argon, but when the Mg loses 2 electrons it will have the same electronic structure as neon, meaning the pair don't match.

Question 15: D

Don't get confused – this is actually easy since background radiation has been corrected for.
Source X has a half-life of 4.8 hours and thus has 5 half-lives in 24 hours.
$Activity\ of\ X\ =\ 320\ x\ 0.5^5\ =\ 320\ x\frac{1}{32} = 10$
Source Y has a half-life of 8 hours and thus has 3 half-lives in 24 hours.
$Activity\ of\ Y\ =\ 480\ x\ 0.5^3 = 480\ x\frac{1}{8} =\ 60$
$Total\ Activity\ =\ 60\ +\ 10\ =\ 70$

Question 16: D

Start off by writing the relationships mathematically: $x\ \alpha\ z^2\ and\ y\ \alpha\ \frac{1}{z^3}$
Now make the powers equivalent so we can substitute: $x^3\ \alpha\ z^6\ and\ y^2\ \alpha\ \frac{1}{z^6}$
$So\ y^2\ \alpha\ \frac{1}{x^3}\ and\ x^3\ \alpha\ \frac{1}{y^2}$

Question 17: A

This question requires knowledge of somatic cell nuclear transfer. 2 is incorrect, because this procedure doesn't involve sperm cells. 4 is also incorrect, because the egg with the newly transferred nucleus must begin to divide, and not differentiate (point 1). The other 3 points are valid.

Question 18: E

$NaOH + HCl \rightarrow NaCl + H_2O$
The atomic mass of NaOH = 23 + 16 + 1 = 40
Theoretical maximum of NaOH in sample: $\frac{1.2}{40}$ = 0.03
Moles of NaOH in sample that react is given by $n = cV$:
$\frac{50}{1000}$ x 0.5 = 0.025
Purity: $\frac{0.025}{0.03}$ = $\frac{5}{6}$ = 83.3%

Question 19: D
Recall that Power = IV = I^2R. Since the resistors are in series, the overall current is given by: $I = \frac{V}{R1+R2}$

Thus, Power = $(\frac{V}{R1+R2})^2 R1 = \frac{V^2 R1}{(R1+R2)^2}$

Question 20: D

Smallest Cube:
We have 5 faces of the smaller shape, which is 5 x 1= **5 cm^2**

Middle Cube:
Where the small cube joins the middle cube, we have a right angled triangle with lengths x, x and 1. Using Pythagoras: $1^2 = x^2 + x^2 = 2x^2$
$x = \sqrt{\frac{1}{2}} = \frac{\sqrt{2}}{2}$.
Since the triangle makes up half the side, the total length of the side = $\sqrt{2}$
There are 4 faces fully uncovered and one face partially covered by the smaller shape. Thus, the surface area = $4 \times \sqrt{2} \times \sqrt{2}$ = 8
Surface area of top face = $\sqrt{2} \times \sqrt{2}$ – 1 = 1
Surface Area of 2nd layer = 8 + 1= **9 cm^2**

Largest Cube:

Using Pythagoras again: $\sqrt{2}^2 = x^2 + x^2 = 2x^2$

$2x^2 = 2$

$Thus, x = 1$. Since the triangle makes up half the side, the total length of the side = 2.

There are 5 faces fully uncovered and one face partially covered by the smaller shape. Thus, the surface area = $5 \times 2 \times 2 = 20$

Surface area of top face = $2 \times 2 - 2 = 2$

Surface Area of 3rd layer = $20 + 2 = $ **22 cm^2**

Total Surface Area: $5 + 9 + 22 = $ **36 cm^2**

Question 21: E

The entire genome is found in every cell in the body, hence 1 and 2 are correct. Starch is broken down before it reaches the liver so 3 is incorrect.

Question 22: C

There are 2 atoms of Cr in the equation, so **d** must be 2. The equation must balance for charge, so **b** must be 8. Comparing **a** and **c** shows that these coefficients change the number of oxygens only and do not affect the number of carbons or hydrogens. Thus to have the correct number of hydrogens, **e** must be 4. **a** and **c** are 3, but this does not have to be deduced in this question.

Question 23: D

A. Rearrangement of $F = ma$
B. Rearrangement of $V = IR$
C. Rearrangement of $E_k = \dfrac{mv^2}{2}$
D. The relationship between wavelength and frequency is given by: $v = f\lambda$. If the y axis was wavelength, the axis should be $\dfrac{1}{f}$ i.e. the inverse of frequency (not a direct correlation).
E. Rearrangement of $Work\ Done = Force \times Distance$

Question 24: C

We need to calculate the probability of either:

➤ 2 blue balls and 1 red ball
➤ 2 red balls and 1 blue ball

Each combination has 3 permutations (i.e. the first combination can be BBR or BRB or RBB).

Probability of 2 Blue Balls $= \frac{8}{10} \, x \, \frac{7}{9} \, x \, \frac{2}{8} \, x \, 3 = \frac{336}{720}$

Probability of 2 Red Balls $= \frac{2}{10} \, x \, \frac{1}{9} \, x \, \frac{8}{8} \, x \, 3 = \frac{48}{720}$

Total Probability $= \frac{48}{720} + \frac{336}{720}$

$\frac{384}{720} = \frac{8}{15}$

Question 25: C

Let's call the dominant allele A and the recessive allele a. We're looking for the proportion of Aa cats. 50% in the first cross, and 67% in the second (dead organisms don't contribute to a population).

	A	a
A	Aa $(\frac{1}{4})$	aa $(\frac{1}{4})$
A	Aa $(\frac{1}{4})$	aa $(\frac{1}{4})$

	A	a
A	AA (dead)	Aa $(\frac{1}{3})$
a	Aa $(\frac{1}{3})$	aa $(\frac{1}{3})$

Question 26: B

3, then 6.
As a catalyst is not used up in the reaction, we can see that using 3 then 6 uses NO to speed up the reaction but then replenishes it at the end. We can also see that a by-product which is not present in the net production, NO_2, is used up before the final products are formed.
Finally, the reagents used which are used up at SO_2 and ½ O_2 as seen in the reaction, and SO_3 is the only net product generated.

Question 27: E

The kinetic energy is given by $\frac{mv^2}{2}$ i.e. $\frac{4v^2}{2} = 1800$.

Thus, $v = 30$ ms^{-1}

Using $F = ma$, the current acceleration is $= \frac{20}{4} = 5\ ms^{-2}$

Now calculate the velocity after 2 seconds of acceleration by the same force by using: $v = u + at$: $v = 30 + 2 \times 5 = 40$

Then calculate the final kinetic energy: $\frac{4 \times 40^2}{2} = 3200$ J.

Finally, the extra kinetic energy is the difference between 3200 and 1800 = 1400 J

END OF SECTION

Section 3

"When you want to know how things really work, study them when they are coming apart." (William Gibson)

➤ This statement suggests that the function of a system is not fully represented when it is working smoothly, rather it is only when the system is put under stressful conditions that the intricacies and factors in the system can be fully appreciated. This concept can be appreciated from a tangible example of a working system, such as the internal structures in a clock. When certain cogs in the clock fall out or stop working, it is easy to identify their place in the overall system. This follows the suggestion by the phrase that a functioning system can mask certain important properties that the system possesses. A system 'coming apart' allows identification of different parts, their purposes and their importance with regards to the function of the whole system. This can be represented by the mutation of certain genes leading to defects, such as in the case of cystic fibrosis, the mutation in the chloride channel shows its vital involvement in the secretion of mucus. In addition, 'coming apart' can help identify the original function of the system, as it will presumably be unable to perform it under those conditions.

➤ This method for studying systems does however have flaws. If the entire representation of the system is based on the lack of function of the system, this means that in some cases, the original function of cannot be understood. The use of such a principle therefore relies heavily on background knowledge, as without some understanding of the system, its lack of function could mean very little. For example, a certain part of a computer can malfunction, leading to a complete breakdown; however, without understanding the basics of what each part in the computer provides to the function, there will be too many unknowns to really build up an understanding. Additionally, if more than one factor leads to the coming apart of the system, a more subtle function of a part could be masked by a less subtle function of another.

➤ This method also underestimates the complexity of the system and the number of factors that may be interacting. It also does not allow you to appreciate the system as a whole.

➤ Overall, this method could be applicable in a simple system that there is already basic knowledge in place. However, for a more complex system that includes the involvement of a number of parts, or a system that has yet to be investigated, it may not accurately represent all the interacting features.

Good surgeons should be encouraged to take on tough cases, not just safe, routine ones. Publishing an individual surgeon's mortality rates may have the opposite effect.

➤ Tough cases present a challenge to surgeons, as increased difficulty of the procedure leads to an increased risk of mortality. It is therefore suggested that due to this increased likelihood of mortality, doctors may be reluctant to take tough cases on if the records were public as their reputation would be somewhat tarnished if the operations were unsuccessful. Public exposure of surgical league tables could also prevent consent from certain patients for certain surgeons to carry out procedures. In particular, certain cases of high mortality rates in surgeons could show that the surgeon is more experienced as they have performed in situations of increased risk. The surgeon could also feel increased pressure in certain procedures, leading to potential negative outcomes. This league table could also undermine the expertise of both the GMC and the hospital, which must make regular reviews of their doctors to make sure that they are working to the best of their abilities. In addition, mortality rates give very little information about the situation in which the death took place and in a number of cases, it could have no reflection on the surgeon at all.

➢ Publishing mortality rates could also have a positive impact on surgeons. I suggested above that this could put the surgeons under increased pressure, however all doctors should feel a certain pressure as they have a responsibility to the patient. In the case of the surgeon, they hold patient's life in their hands and they should not forget that they are obligated to perform to the best of their ability. Slightly contrastingly, a league table should have no impact on the performance of a doctor, as a doctor must always act with the patient's best interest at heart, rather than worrying about their reputation. Patients also have a right to know the performance record of a doctor, as they are putting their welfare into their hands, and therefore have a right to know all the factors and risks involved in making such a decision, including their surgeon.

➢ To use such a league table for the improvement of surgical performance would be extremely beneficial; however it is unlikely that this would be the case. It is more likely that there will be a negative impact on surgical performance, or even the decision to perform the surgery in the first place. In conclusion it is probably more beneficial for both the surgeon and the patient that the league table be kept private, as it enables the doctors to act as they see fit, potentially saving more lives due to the undertaking of riskier but more beneficial operations.

"Ignorance more frequently begets confidence than does knowledge: it is those who know little, and not those who know much, who so positively assert that this or that problem will never be solved by science." (Charles Darwin)

➢ Darwin is suggesting that people who know very little about science are very confident that they know the limits of the field and therefore do not think it is able to make progress in certain areas. This can be valid idea in certain respects as little knowledge of a subject can cause a person to think they know the important aspects of a certain field. It might however actually be the case that the field has much more complexities that can offer very exciting potential developments, something which could be overlooked by an ignorant person.

➤ This concept can be represented by a self-diagnosis made by a patient online, they are only being exposed to very superficial (and potentially incorrect) areas of the field and this can lead them to incorrect conclusions.

➤ On the contrary this concept does not always apply. When looking at research environments, it is possible for a very knowledgeable researcher to have studied the subject for such an extended period of time that their sense of the bigger picture becomes clouded. This could mean that an ignorant person is then able to come and have a different take on the problem, as they have not developed the same mind-set of the knowledgeable researcher and they are less aware of possible limitations of the field, able to look 'outside the box'.

➤ This can be compared to a partnership between a engineer and a biologist in the development of medical equipment, the engineer might not know very much about biology, they are however able to give a different outlook on the problem. Similarly a scientist very knowledgeable in a field may not be able to accept that the field may be unable to progress, something that an ignorant person may be able to notice. There is also the possibility that an ignorant person may assume that science has not limits, which can be helpful and detrimental depending on the situation.

➤ Overall, this attitude does have some truth, I find however that it is cynical and a generalisation. It does not take into account that it is new and possibly initially ignorant minds that are pushing the boundaries of science, allowing it progress at a rapid pace.

In a world where we struggle to feed an ever-expanding human population, owning pets cannot be justified.

➢   This phrase suggests that the expense of owning a pet is unnecessary, rather the resources used to support a pet should be used to help support the over-expanding population. This argument is based on a number of assumptions and I will attempt to sort through them here.

➢   On one hand, it is true that the population is 'over-expanding' and we have a moral obligation to support those in need. It is also true that ownership of a pet requires a lot of resources. The pet must be fed, watered and housed appropriately. This therefore suggests that the owner must have food and money available for this particular purpose. One could argue that the money spent on the pet and the food that it consumes, could be better used elsewhere. If the resources used to support the pet were dedicated to support the needs of the expanding population, it is possible that a significant positive contribution to the cause could be made. In addition, one could argue that some expensive and exotic pets are an unnecessary luxury and too indulgent.

➢   On the other hand, the above statement assumes that the resources and food supplied to pets could be better used elsewhere. Owning a pet is an individual's decision, a choice to spend their money how they please. There is also no guarantee that even if these owners did not own a pet they would spend the equivalent amount supporting those in need, they might instead buy something equivalently recreational.

➢   An extrapolation of the above statement might lead one to say "why don't we restrict television sales and other such luxuries as the funds could be better used elsewhere?" As further support against this statement, it is important to consider the importance of pet ownership, such as the life-saving duties of guide dogs, likely to be considered a worthwhile expense. In addition, ownership of pets in some cases can reduce the wastage due to their consumption of leftover food, which would have been otherwise discarded.

➢ Additionally, the money spent on pets can be a form of support for the economy. A stronger economy allows the government to provide more assistance to those in need.

➢ In conclusion, we have a moral obligation to help those in need, however, pet ownership and lack of resources for an expanding population are not necessarily correlated, as the ownership cannot account the a massive resource deficit. Making steps to prevent food wastage or encouraging charitable donations may be a more worthwhile venture.

END OF PAPER

Afterword

Remember that the route to a high score is your approach and practice. Don't fall into the trap that *"you can't prepare for the BMAT"*– this couldn't be further from the truth. With knowledge of the test, time-saving techniques and plenty of practice you can dramatically boost your score.

Work hard, never give up and do yourself justice.

Good luck!

Acknowledgements

Thanks must go *Somil* for his tremendous help in putting these set of answers together and to *David* for lending his expertise with the trickiest of questions.

About UniAdmissions

UniAdmissions is an educational consultancy that specialises in supporting **applications to Medical School and to Oxbridge**.

Every year, we work with hundreds of applicants and schools across the UK. From free resources to our *Ultimate Guide Books* and from intensive courses to bespoke individual tuition – with a team of **300 Expert Tutors** and a proven track record, it's easy to see why UniAdmissions is the **UK's number one admissions company**.

We also run an **access scheme** that provides disadvantaged students with free support. To find out more about our support like intensive **BMAT courses** and **BMAT tuition**, check out **www.uniadmissions.co.uk/bmat**

THE ULTIMATE
UKCAT GUIDE
1000
PRACTICE QUESTIONS

✓ Fully Worked Solutions   ✓ Includes All 5 Sections
✓ Time Saving Techniques   ✓ Score Boosting Strategies

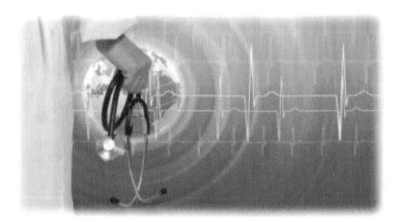

2016 ENTRY

David Salt
Rohan Agarwal

UniAdmissions

www.uniadmissions.co.uk/ukcat-book

THE ULTIMATE BMAT GUIDE

600

PRACTICE QUESTIONS

- ✓ Fully Worked Solutions
- ✓ Time Saving Techniques
- ✓ 10 Annotated Essays
- ✓ Score Boosting Strategies

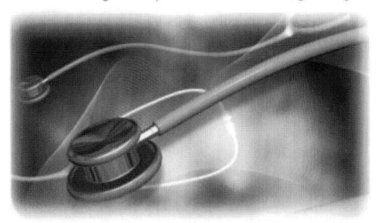

2016 ENTRY

Rohan Agarwal

UniAdmissions

www.uniadmissions.co.uk/bmat-book

THE ULTIMATE
OXBRIDGE
INTERVIEW GUIDE

✓ Worked Answers   ✓ 18 Subjects
✓ 900 Past Questions   ✓ Expert Advice

2016 ENTRY

Rohan Agarwal

UniAdmissions

www.uniadmissions.co.uk/oxbridge-interview-book

BMAT INTENSIVE COURSE

If you're looking to improve your BMAT score in a short space of time, our **BMAT intensive course** is perfect for you. It's a fully interactive seminar that guides you through sections 1, 2 and 3 of the BMAT.

You are taught by our experienced BMAT experts, who are Doctors or senior Oxbridge medical tutors who excelled in the BMAT. The aim is to teach you powerful time-saving techniques and strategies to help you succeed for test day.

➢ Full Day intensive Course
➢ Guaranteed Small Groups [Max 12 Students per Tutor]
➢ 4 Full Practice Papers (Worth £ 60)
➢ A copy of our "The Ultimate BMAT Guide" (Worth £ 30)
➢ Expert BMAT Essay Marking
➢ Ongoing Tutor Support until Test date – never be alone again.

Timetable:
➢ **1030 - 1200:** Section 1
➢ **1200 - 1300:** Section 2
➢ **1300 - 1330:** Lunch
➢ **1330 - 1415:** Section 2
➢ **1415 - 1445:** Section 3
➢ **1500 - 1700:** Mock Test
➢ **1710 - 1750:** Mock Test Debrief
➢ **1750 - 1800:** Questions

Bookings for 2015 open on 15th June and courses are held in *London, Birmingham, Manchester and Leeds* throughout September + October.

The course is normally £175 but you can get £25 off by using the code "*BMATPPS25*" at checkout.

www.uniadmissions.co.uk/bmat-course

MEDICINE INTERVIEW COURSE

If you've got an upcoming interview for medical school – this is the perfect course for you. You get individual attention throughout the day and are taught by Oxbridge tutors + senior doctors on how to approach the medical interview.

- ➤ Full Day intensive Course
- ➤ Guaranteed Small Groups
- ➤ 4 Hours of Small group teaching
- ➤ 2 x 30 minute individual Mock Interviews + Written Feedback
- ➤ Full MMI interview circuit with written feedback
- ➤ Ongoing Tutor Support until your interview – never be alone again

Timetable:
- ➤ **1000 - 1015:** Registration
- ➤ **1015 - 1030:** Talk: Key to interview Success
- ➤ **1030 - 1130:** Tutorial: Common Interview Questions
- ➤ **1145 - 1245:** 2 x Individual Mock Interviews
- ➤ **1245 - 1330:** Lunch
- ➤ **1330 - 1430:** Medical Ethics Workshop
- ➤ **1445 - 1545:** MMI Circuit
- ➤ **1600 - 1645:** Situational Judgement Workshop
- ➤ **1645 - 1730:** Debrief and Finish

Bookings for 2015 open on 15th September and courses are held in *London*, throughout November + December.

The course is normally £295 but you can get £35 off by using the code *"BMATPPS35"* at checkout.

www.uniadmissions.co.uk/medical-school-interview-course

£35 VOUCHER:
BMATPPS35

NOTES

NOTES

13605801R00153

Printed in Great Britain
by Amazon.co.uk, Ltd.,
Marston Gate.